BODY GEOGRAPHIC

AMERICAN LIVES   Series editor: Tobias Wolff

Body Geographic

Barrie Jean Borich

University of Nebraska Press : Lincoln and London

Acknowledgments for previously published material appear on page 246, which constitutes an extension of the copyright page.

Library of Congress Cataloging-in-Publication Data
Borich, Barrie Jean, 1959–
Body geographic / Barrie Jean Borich.
pages cm. —(American lives)
Includes bibliographical references.
ISBN 978-0-8032-3985-2 (paper: alkaline paper)
1. Borich, Barrie Jean, 1959– 2. Borich, Barrie Jean, 1959—Childhood and youth. 3. Authors, American—20th century—Biography. 4. Lesbian authors—United States—Biography. 5. Self-perception in women. 6. Women—Sexual behavior—Psychological aspects. 7. Mind and body. 8. Maps—Psychological aspects. 9. Middle West—Geography—Psychological aspects. 10. Middle West—Biography. I. Title.
PS3552.07529Z46 2013
818'.5403—dc23   2012030607

Set in Scala by Laura Wellington.
Designed by Ashley Muehlbauer.

For my father, who offered the city and a map.

FIG. 1. *Americam utramque: aliis correctiorem* by G. van Keulen, 1700s.

I wake from dreams of a city
like no other, the bright city
of beauty I thought I'd lost
when I lost my faith that one day
we would come into our lives.

PHILIP LEVINE, *The Rat of Faith*

FIG. 2. *Map of Europe as Queen* by Sebastian Munster, 1570.

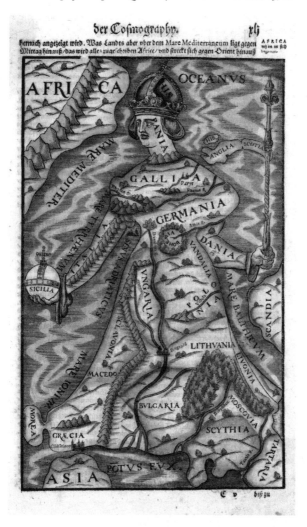

The Croats, Poles, Bohemians, Prussians, and Italians
of my family fled the belly of Queen Europe. Our
American story is an atlas of the bodies we became.

Contents of My New and Accurate Atlas

BODY GEOGRAPHIC

FIG. 3. *American Progress* by John Gast, 1872.

The big blond body of Miss Manifest Destiny,
dragging America into the middle.

My Body as the Middle West

SCALE: The measure of one woman's body = the distance between two cities.

The Body

I am facedown on the table as he needles my lower back. The tattoo gun hums and my neck and shoulders clench. Though I can't see him, I feel his presence, behind me.

The pain maps I consulted told me this tattoo should not hurt as much as it does. I don't remember such sharp pain with the others—the leopard on my shoulder, the amber rose on my ankle, the blossoming branch on my forearm. Yet I am not crying. I am not moving. I am trying to vanish into this wash, which I do, for long pauses that end abruptly.

As he works I can't help but notice how unusual it is for me to be so close to a man. I am a woman who prefers women, have been married to Linnea now for over two decades, have not been this intimate with a dude in years. Ordinarily such proximity to anyone I don't know makes me nervous. I'm not one to get a massage. I warm slowly to new chiropractors and doctors. I was slow to learn the Minnesota hug, though have an easier time hugging women than men. A man

3

leaning over my exposed backside is not typical in my day-to-day, but tattoos are boundary-breaking situations. This new charting, across my middle, in more than one way remaps me.

But the work he's doing hurts. Just as I begin to consider rearing up and slapping the tattoo gun out of his hand, he finally lifts the needle. This rush of absence feels like love.

The Map

One drunken night when I was newly in love, my then-lover and I stood in a public restroom in South Minneapolis, looking into a streaked mirror. I stared at my own face with the devotion of the drunken and whispered to my lover that my eyes, nose, and mouth looked to me like a map. It was the sort of thing my lover liked to talk about. That woman's face looks like a map of Eastern Europe, she'd say about some stunningly unconventional beauty or other we'd meet in passing, and I must have wished her to say the same about me. We were young—me only twenty-three—and often drunk or stoned and prone to believe all manner of unlikely things about our lives in our mostly women's new world, the lesbian nation, a floating country with invisible borders that my lover, nine years older than I, had arrived at first. I suppose I was trying to impress her, trying to get her to see me better, and indeed I was pleased when she nodded and told me she did see it too, my face made from the copper stones of some beautiful old country.

Neither of us had been yet to our family's old countries. I hadn't yet even been away from the Western hemisphere. Drunk as I was that night, if I made out anything in that wavy approximation of my features, l likely saw my father, whom I resemble. If I saw a map it was probably just that of my dad's and my Chicago, with perhaps some cast of my grandfather's and great-grandfather's Croatia underneath. I was taking note then of not so much ground truth as history, one of so many twentieth-century migration stories that started in the dregs and stones of an impoverished Balkan village and continued in the steel mill regions of the American middle.

My lover was a short Jewish woman with curly black hair, recently migrated from Boston, resettling here in the Scandinavian upper Midwest to work at the feminist theater company where we met, her homesickness the reason she talked about maps. I was not nearly so far from home, a tall blond native midwesterner just one major metropolis west of the city where I was born. And yet the idea of the map, that my body might carry a geography of memory, stayed with me from that night forward.

Years later I would read, in a book about the history of mapping, that maps are less actualities than acts of discernment. And yes, this is what I was doing looking into that mirror—discerning my asymmetrical 1980s haircut, the smudge of eyeliner under my eyes, the way my body had just begun to feel itself in love, in sex, yes, finally present for a lover in ways I hadn't been with the women and men who had come before. But also I had begun to locate myself in time and place. When I said my face was a map I meant that I was beginning to discern what I'd decided to make of myself, mapping as the act of making out some new and more accurate self that I hadn't made out before.

The Middle

Some tattoos hurt more than others. The less flesh, the more pain. Fatty areas, like the upper arm, buffer better, but at parts of the back, the ankle, elbow, and hip, the bone is too close to the skin. And the black ink hurts more than the colors. Today, the first day's work on my back, the ink is all black. I've asked the artist to make me a map of urban architecture, of infrastructure, and he's providing.

But this pain in my lower back as he works is somehow more than pain, which has to do, I think, with the vulnerabilities of the woman's middle. When men call tattoos on the female sacral area the *tramp stamp* their word choice is obviously misogynistic, but hatred tends to gravitate toward wounds. My body has areas much more intimate than the lower back and yet, as he needles, the pain undulates up my belly to my throat.

Linnea has been sitting to one side of the action, one of her heavy boots balanced on the ledge of the ornamental fishpond at the center of the tattoo parlor. She leans on one leg to watch the giant koi bubble up and down in their brick canal. When we first met, Linnea kept a tank in her bedroom, and for as long as I've known her she's loved domesticated fish. But now she must see some new sting cross my face, enough to pull her away from the pond. She takes off her heavy motorcycle jacket and scrapes a chair up close, to hold my hand, but the distraction is too sweet, the press of her fingers cloying. I do and don't want to be distracted.

Middles are both solid and vulnerable. In the famous 1872 landscape painting by William Gast called *American Progress* the middle of the New World is traversed by a big blond archetypal female. In the painting Columbia floats across the center, what was then, in the late nineteenth century, called the Middle West, both a middle and a frontier. The burned middle plains graze Columbia's pale toe. Miss Manifest Destiny is heading for Hollywood, clothed in a white sheet that flaps behind her like a ripped flag, the fabric falling off her left breast, exposing her nipple to the hard wind. This is the myth of the middle, an empty space waiting to be strung up with electric wires, its undesirables vanquished and vanished. The woman's body can stand in for a fantasy of American habitation only if she is assumed to have no inhabiting desires of her own.

To conquer a country you have to trample the middle. We all hunch over to cradle our losses, to protect from the coming kick. The middle is a pivot where we remake careers, relocate homes, abandon or revive marriages, decide whether to stay or go. I desire. I long to inhabit. My middle is made of overlays the tattoo needle unpeels.

The City

Once, sleeping deeply after spending a bit too long in a historical archive—where I'd peered into map after map of Croatia, Poland, Bohemia, and Chicago, deciphered charts of countries with arrows accounting for which old European population moved to which new American city, read transcripts of interviews with early twentieth-century immigrants who came to the industrial Midwest to work in the steel mills, not at all sure what I was looking for—I dreamed I took a trolley tour of some city. It was the prototype Great Lakes port city, built by immigrants like my great-grandfather Big Petar. The trolley tour guide told us we were about to see the city tourists never saw, and then the train clamored up steps and through eroded alleyways. We trundled past working docks and through the center of restaurants where lovers leaned together or walked encircled in one another's arms. Then we rumbled outside again, into a frantic intersection of street vendors, crowded, as in archival photos of the old Maxwell Street Market in Chicago.

When I found myself on foot I was caught in the center of a full-color twenty-first-century throng, Chicago's State Street right before Christmas, except now and then I noticed a filmy historical body brushing past, dressed in early twentieth-century garb, as if I'd spotted a cartoon character in the background of a news documentary, bodies of the past jumbled up with the bodies of the present, transparent men in hats, bustled women holding children's hands and avoiding the eyes of strangers. The past and the present were strips of black-and-white film stock, the street a palimpsest, mingling and simultaneous. This was what I longed for, I realized when I woke. A map I could inhabit, a city tangibly conscious of the city that had come before.

Maps within the Map

Maps obscure more than they reveal because their flatness is contrary to the layered experience of living. Maps are representational, but life is lived in the body, is dimensional, has voice and history. So every map can't help but contain other maps, areas of detail requiring special attention, even when the insets don't show. The body, my body, is a stacked atlas of memory. If we think the middle of our lives are flat we mistake surface for substance.

The Geography

The actual woman's body in the middle of her life is neither map nor archetype, is both settlement and frontier. I choose, now, at age fifty, to treat the surface of my back as a cartographer's canvas. I stretch out on the tattooing table. My body clutches and shivers. The artist inks a dual city skyline. My Chicago in the center. My Minneapolis to either side. The infrastructure of that sharp black ink stings worse than I imagined it could. Linnea squeezes my hand, but again I shoo her away. I came here to pull all my maps to the surface, not just a drunk girl's hallucination this time, but a marking more permanent. Of course it hurts when he maps me in my history.

FIG. 4. *The Man of Commerce* by A. F. McKay, 1889.

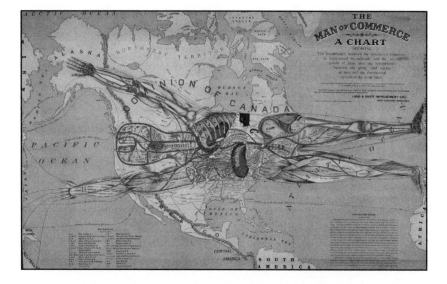

The road map of the middle could be mistaken for capillaries
and veins, just as migration is often confused with change.

MAP 1

Geographical Solutions

A map of the Middle West, with
insets past and current

The Amtrak depot was cold, which was why I wondered about the young blond woman across the waiting room from me wearing sequined flip-flops, her arms bare. She looked to be the age of the college freshmen I'd taught the previous spring. Wasn't she chilly in this dank station?

I'd noticed her earlier as well, because her sweatshirt and pants were so sharply green that I'd almost had to squint to look. I tend to take note of girls her age, young women with slight bodies and cagey faces, because of how they shock me back to who I was at nineteen. Now, on a rainy September morning, in this featureless warehouse gully of Saint Paul, the girl had stripped down to a thin tank top. How could she be hot in this drafty station, when the heat still hadn't been turned on for the season? But I forgot about her as we all lined up to board the train.

The *Empire Builder* is the name of this passenger line on the west-to-midwest route along the northern plains. It runs from Puget Sound to Chicago, stopping on the way in this Saint Paul industrial park. A double-decker Amtrak cruiser with curved and weather-splotched observation-car windows, the *Empire Builder* is not just one train but a fleet of four—two traveling west, two east—passing each other in the long silence of Montana and North Dakota. Narrow headlight beams intersect in the middle of the night on the far western segment of the route, the whoosh of speed catching for a moment in the vacuum of their passing, lives echoing each other in the occasionally lit-up windows, passengers up late drinking or reading or staring out, until the whoosh resumes and the meeting is over with a spark, a clank, a long whistle's moan into the dark.

I always cringe when I hear the stationmaster announce this train's name. I hate all those parts of American history that are about rounding up the natives and making way for progress. The Empire Builder was the nickname of the nineteenth-century Saint Paul railroad magnate James J. Hill, and this train was named in homage to the roots of development frenzy, when train tracks wrapped the continent in a leash of steel that must have made the old coot lean back in his chair, rub his one good eye, and think, *Mine, mine, mine*.

Yet all Americans, even the most put-upon among us, might have a little bit of empire building in our makeup, some desire to refind the lost parts of ourselves through locating and owning, landing somewhere and inscribing our names. I recognize the baser version of the urge when I come across stuff I want, from a loft with a view in my home city of Chicago to a sweater with a low neckline I know will cause Linnea to kiss my collarbone. *Mine*. This blank pull of wanting, a desire to erase all obstacles, can reel me into one of those give-that-girl-a-crown-and-a-bundle-of-roses daydreams, the girly version of James J. Hill's long recline back in a leather chair as cigar smoke forms a crown just above his head.

Boarding the train to Chicago, I was trying to pinpoint what it was I meant to regain on this trip back, when behind me someone yelled. Hey! We need help over here. I turned to see that underdressed blond girl again. Pale to begin with, she had blanched gray-white, her eyes unfocused, her thin body slouched on the shoulders of two mom-like middle-aged women with hair pulled back into ponytails. These women had probably been looking forward to curling up on the train and sleeping at least until Wisconsin Dells, and now they had this kid—they didn't seem to know her—hanging off their shoulders, loose-limbed as a straw girl.

The line moved forward, out of the station and toward the platform, but when I looked back a few moments later the girl was lying down flat on the floor. Her feet had fallen askew. A silver ring glinted dully from one of her wan toes. A paunchy stationmaster with thinning hair leaned over her, shouting, Are you conscious? Can you hear me? Even though the guy was yelling, he sounded calm, unruffled, almost bored, taking care of his daily routine. The women who had been holding up the girl crouched around her now, as if they were conducting a séance. The stationmaster called an ambulance on his walkie-talkie. Was the girl having a seizure? Maybe she hadn't eaten yet this morning. Maybe she hadn't eaten in a week. She was skinny enough to be bulimic.

There was nothing for the rest of us to do; already too many people were crowding around the fallen girl. The stationmaster asked folks to please step forward. We boarded the train, most of us craning our heads back twice, three times, to gawk.

This kind of thing, skinny blond girls fainting in broad daylight, is always happening on or around Amtrak. It might be something about the train, a long container of change that compresses people together, as in the plot of a 1970s disaster movie, all those lives that wouldn't otherwise intersect stuck together behind a smoke-spewing engine dragging them across the prairie. Still I sometimes take Amtrak back to Chicago because I like the train and don't like planes and because the train helps me remember times past, when I was a skinny, fallen blond girl myself.

On this trip, if anyone had asked, I would have said I was traveling home to see a show by the photographer Terry Evans, a series of large-scale aerial portraits of the city and its suburbs, exhibited outdoors, in the Loop's new Millennium Park. But I was also homesick. As long as Linnea and I had been together, nearly twenty years, and despite all practical home and work considerations, I'd been wishing we'd leave Minneapolis and move back to Chicago, and lately my longings had gotten worse. Evans's panoramas of the urban prairie, shot from such untouchable heights, photographs I'd so far seen only in books, felt both familiar and strange. The shift in visual position recast the broken whole as beautiful, and the photographs became like mirrors held up to parts of my body nobody in Minnesota could see. This personal terrain—the histories gone missing in me but then seen anew—was what I sought each time I ventured back to Chicago. I wanted some key to discern the difference between what, in Alcoholics Anonymous, we describe as the things we can change and the things we cannot.

Though Linnea and I are not morning people, she was good to me this early Sunday, waking at 5 a.m. to get me to the depot an hour before departure. She had even come into the station, her curly gray hair mussed, one sweatpants leg shoved up a little higher than the other. She'd waited with me for more than an hour, the train late again, though I was lousy company, griping about stiff seats, hard lights, and the nonexistence of the bullet train between Minneapolis and Chicago that was supposed to have been built by now, the one that promised to whisk passengers between my two cities in three hours, which pretty soon would be the amount of time I'd been waiting for this blasted *Empire Builder*.

HALT. Years back, when I first quit drinking, the AA old-timers warned me about hours like these, when I'd find myself hungry, angry, lonely, tired. HALT is what they called it. Acronyms and slogans are big in AA, and some of them are silly, but this one has always made sense to me. Stop moving forward. Pay attention. Wake up before you take another step. The idea is to stop you before you take a drink, which wasn't a big danger in that nothing train station so early in the morning, but in my case HALT was also a warning to change direction before I had to be sorry later for something I'd done or said to Linnea. HALT is one of the ways I usually remember to live since moving away from Chicago.

The train takes at least eight hours to get to its terminus, if we don't stop and sit somewhere in the Wisconsin brush. I like to watch, from the train windows, the shifts between Minneapolis and Chicago, the seismic recalculation, a remaking caused by the slow, ravaging route the glaciers took, by centuries of immigration, by the transformation of the prairie into the American farm.

When I was the age of that girl we left on the station floor, I did things on trains that I have trouble understanding today, risky things I thought would make me happy, like making out all night with an off-duty conductor on the line running west back to Chicago from Syracuse, and time-wasting things, like spending an hour in an onboard ladies' room lounge with a glaze-eyed redhead recruiting for the est seminars she promised would free me from the past, transform me into a human who was cleaner and better than I could ever expect to be.

Even on this trip I found myself doing things I'd never do on land, as when I sat still and smiled while a very thuggish, very young man in the adjoining seat told me he was on his way into the city for his day in court and then tried to pick me up. I've been known to tell complete strangers minute details about my life, but I told this young man nothing. I wanted to avoid getting stuck on the train next to a guy who might turn out to be a homophobe who knew too much about me.

It's volatile enough that so many on the train, in the Midwest at least, are people already in trouble, possibly lost, some so close to combustion that one thing or another is bound to blow the minute they sit down for an hour or more, hoping to get away, hoping to arrive in a far better place. There's always the danger, on the way there, of falling off or down or through, of never arriving at the alabaster city. Which was why I kept muttering the words the stationmaster had shouted into that fainting girl's ear: *Are you conscious?* I had long been whispering the same question to myself.

Inset of the Imitation City

People, 28 million, from all over, poured out of the Chicago train depots in 1893. They came to look at the alabaster city. The alabaster city is a name for Chicago, or a part of Chicago, the imitation city of projected desire, the fake alabaster skyline, called also the White City, built on the South Side for the 1893 Columbian Exposition.

The world's fair featured statues of bare-breasted ladies who were supposed to symbolize late nineteenth-century Empire Builder America, staring over the temporary capitol like pirate captains, chanting with voices I imagine as a cross between Lauren Bacall and the Greek Sirens, *Progress, Progress, Progress.* If every city is both a real place and a dream place, our expectations catch in our throats as we look up at the heights and the lights.

The white buildings of the world's fair were as long as the fields these visitors plowed back in Indiana. The central plaza featured statues with bosoms bigger than cow heads, waterways wider than the harbors back in the Old Country, fountains with Our Lady Columbia at the center, surrounded by water spouting taller than the rock ridges along Lake Superior's shore, back up in Michigan mining territory. Those who came stood on ferries, on overlooks, and they stared and stared, as if they were viewing ancient Athens. But this was someplace new.

The alabaster city was Chicago's dream of itself. Most of those people, not just Chicagoans, must have known the White City was a phony—a vacation park, an extravaganza, the real city's mythic twin—but they didn't care. They were looking for the technology of completion, some shimmer of a future freed from the past.

The White City was made of 120,000 incandescent lights, 18,000 tons of iron and steel, 75 million feet of lumber, and 30,000 tons of wall plaster. The Ferris wheel had cars the size of train engines. This was at the cusp of the twentieth century—before machine-made wars and atrocities sullied America's technological optimism—the time of intellectuals like Henry Adams, who thought we might replace the Madonna with the Machine. Katharine Lee Bates wrote about the White City in the song "America the Beautiful." *Thine alabaster cities gleam.* The empire builder's dream of America has always promised that by taking possession of a new place we can repossess ourselves, make our lives over. But the White City was mere intoxication, a touchable mirage, a gorgeous scam, a whitewashed stage set sparking and trilling in the midwestern sun. *Oh beautiful.*

Inset of the City Inside

The frontal blast of the engines, the streaking whistle wail—these were part of the wallpaper of my childhood. A train horn is a memory trigger, my version of Proust's madeleine, the sound transporting me to a physical past where the rail traffic was too constant to be worth anyone's notice. The minor-key pitch of the whistle was what first carried me back to that landscape of trains.

It used to be that I traveled back to Chicago only when my mother or father begged me to attend a graduation or retirement party, showing up reluctantly, leaving much of myself back in Minnesota with my new world of lesbians, oddballs, and dropouts. All the way there and back I felt transparent, stretched clear across the upper prairie, belonging to neither place, not fully occupying the present.

I have a black-and-white photograph my father took when I was twenty-two. In the photograph my hair is braided down the right side of my head, as I wore it then, imitating some singer-songwriter I'd seen on an album jacket. The shutter captures me as I turn back to look at my parents before stepping onto the platform at Chicago's Union Station, on my way back to Minneapolis, wearing the same scowl that appears in all the pictures my dad shot of me during those years. As soon as I was alone on the train I would release my held breath, smile. But before I boarded—surrounded by the Daniel Burnham–designed train station, with migration history swirling past in a hundred configurations, my mother crying, my father pointing that camera at his only daughter—I refused to admit I was leaving anything behind.

Half a dozen years later Linnea and I took a driving trip from Minneapolis up along Lake Superior into Ontario. Our destination was an amethyst mine near the upper Great Lakes, just east of Thunder Bay. In the mid-1980s lesbians loved to talk about the healing power of herbs and stones and crystals. The amethyst was said to be a sobriety stone, and the lilac glint of the raw gem cast a light that read to me as clarity.

I was newly sober. Correction: I had stopped smoking pot and drinking but hadn't really earned the designation *sober*, still trying then what AA terms the precursor to actual change, the easier, softer way. I hadn't yet done rehab, or even AA. I didn't know yet about the work required to get and stay clean. Years later a sober friend would tell me that 90 percent of us relapse at least once. I had yet to take note of when, how, and why I drank, or of why I might want to (and in fact did) drink again. I'd stopped drinking cold, because even though I was still in my twenties, I was sick and scared and didn't know why, and all around me my drinking and drugging friends and lovers were either spinning out or sobering up. I was afraid of being left behind with nothing but a cheap bottle of wine. And then I fell in love, with Linnea, who, I found out soon enough, liked me only when I wasn't drinking. That sobriety could be contained in a stone was just another projection—like the alabaster city—but I was still a believer then.

Mining amethyst is not like mining coal. The mines in Ontario were really just open ground, like a u-pick-'em raspberry field. The amethysts were glassy purple gashes in the rocky Canadian earth. All we had to do was reach in and gather up all that sobriety, I thought, as if serenity were a commodity I could purchase by the pound, as if the simple weight of a pretty rock in my pocket was all it would take to make me change.

But first we had to get there. We'd meant to stay over along the way, on the Lake Superior shore, but it was a weekend night in resort country, and there wasn't a room anywhere. We couldn't find even an open campsite. So we drove on north and reached the Canadian border well after midnight.

When the border patrolman asked our professions, Linnea had a clear response. She was a graduate student, a teacher. I had no clear categories to offer the man. I was a barely published poet, but did he want to scribble this onto his form? Did he want to hear about my last temp job? When he asked me what I did for a living, I stammered and he squinted. I must have looked like a fugitive making an overnight crossing. This aspect of me might be hard to pick out now, unless my tattoos are showing, but then I still had the air of a teen-age delinquent. My hair was bobbed shorter on one side than on the other and streaked unnaturally red, with a band over the ears shaved all the way to the scalp. I wore a tight, short halter that didn't entirely hide my nipples. The patrolman motioned for Linnea to open the back of the truck, and I whispered to her, I should say I'm a stripper. I meant to make her laugh. Instead she pinched me and whispered back: *Shh.* In our early days Linnea was always shushing me.

The guard went through the bags, stopping before each to ask whose. When I claimed a bag he opened every zipper, pawed through clothes, held every herb tincture up to the light. I don't know why he took my word for which bags were mine. Did he just want to touch my underwear? Linnea pinched me again and gave him her best grin, and finally he let us cross over.

Thunder Bay, the second largest city in northern Ontario, is noth-ing like the homey stretches of highway that line upper Minnesota's north shore, with their quaint donut shops and nature-art galleries. The Canadian side of the border is a shipping port and mill center, its industrial identity evident even at 2 a.m. We were relieved to find a street of old-time lit-up signs, their red arrows pointing down from the damp darkness toward a cluster of drive-in motels, the sort of relics that still operated without irony in pockets of the 1980s. The place we stayed, called the Holiday Inn, looked more like a no-tell motel of 1950s noir flicks than the clean and well-lit American chain of the same name. It was a cheap joint with weathered clerks who didn't look twice at two skinny lesbians in leather rancher hats and studded boots. Midnight cowgirls on a sex jaunt wouldn't have been anything new.

The cabin's room was narrow, the front door not more than five sturdy steps from the back windows. The frilly curtains were drawn and we didn't look to see where we were, just stripped down and fell into bed. The air was muggy and close and I covered up with just a sheet.

We were sleeping skin to skin when the siren scream woke us. I clutched the sheet around my chest like a movie starlet. Linnea swore in Italian. She staggered to the windows, pulling open the curtain just in time to catch the tail end of a freight train speeding past, not six feet from the glass. The sad pipes of the locomotive whistled, I pressed the clammy sheet against my chest, and Linnea and I reached for each other in the darkness. We didn't sleep the rest of the night. Newly in love then, I thought my past had been replaced by my present, but the pitch of that whistle carried me home through the back door of Chicago, as if the map itself had folded around my thighs and pulled me down, south of the Great Lakes shipping ports, to a geography of rails, discarded tires, smoke, and broken industrial pilings. Shocked awake this way, I felt as if I'd fallen back to the swarm of a downtown train depot, hiding from my father's camera within the shadows of all the yearning bodies who had come before me and the shadow of my own body as well, as it had been, as it lived in me still. I was no longer merely a grown woman pressed against the body of her lover in a noir motel room, but also an immigrant mingling in a ravine of history with no idea of how to get out again.

In a fully conscious geography, the landscapes of memory loop into and out of the body like the *Empire Builder*, streaming into the West and back again, the whistle flowing behind like a farewell song, a constant circle of departure and return.

The map of the Middle West is geography as solution, the hard yellow sprawl of Chicago surrounded by the spokes of train tracks that seem to, and once did, hold it all together. The city and its hinterlands are interdependent, the farms unable to exist without the city to hawk their harvests, the city unable to exist without grain to store and sell. The *Empire Builder* trundles into and out of Chicago on tracks that were laid to guarantee that all trade from the East and the West had to change trains here. During its heyday up to thirty-seven lines terminated at Union Station.

Alongside these migrations of commerce came the literary arrivals. Take, for instance, Sister Carrie, the creation of the nineteenth-century Indiana writer Theodore Dreiser, who comes to the city drawn by her ambition but finds that her dream of Chicago begins to fade the minute she steps foot into the trouble of the city itself. If I had been among the exclaiming horde—a girl looking for work like Dreiser's Carrie Meeber, or another world's fairgoer trundling into the city's meaty center—then I would have been a woman not so much brave as stubborn enough to take a trip like this alone. I would have been fluttery as the trip began, or as I imagine it begins, on the crowded train platform in Chicago, October 1893. She is the only woman not wearing a hat. The air is tart, but still she perspires. Earlier, on the train, on the way into the city, her dress snagged on a hinge of her seat as she tried to discourage the attentions of the well-dressed but somehow dirty gentleman sitting beside her. She hopes now that the fray along her hem is not too obvious. She doesn't take the train directly to the fair, as some do, but disembarks downtown. The station is polished and capacious. She doesn't shout to see if her voice will echo but wonders if it might. She would have tried if she'd been less alone, or closer to home, but now she doesn't want people to stare. She pushes her way deeper into the station and sees there are so many people that if she did yell out her voice would be absorbed into mounds of cotton clothing, nests of ladies' hats, the flesh of the masses themselves, who suck up particular sounds and replace them with a monosyllabic buzz. This is her first awakening to the actual city: dissonance, static, a cotton-absorbed hum.

Inset of the Rose-Colored City

My dad's mother, Gram Rose, left the Lake Michigan mill plain for the Floridian Gulf Coast at age seventy and by the time she was ninety-five had forgotten most of the actual city, but she never forgot the Chicago she imagined. In Rose's late years the neighbors found her lost on the way back from her walk around the golf course, the old lady with the flyaway hair who ventured out once a day, if it was warm enough, to sun herself along the road in front of her house.

By the time I thought to ask her questions about her old Chicago,

Gram Rose didn't have much to say about the East Side port district where she'd grown up, claiming not to remember anything that might make her look like she'd come from the city's lower depths. Even before the dementia set in, Gram told no stories of growing up on Avenue H, and after she started slipping I heard her proclaim more than once, *I am the last living sister,* even when her youngest and very much still living sibling, my great-aunt Babe, had just been to visit. Babe was the one who told me how their father had lost his toes in a railroad yard accident and how Gram had nearly been kicked out of the South Chicago Hospital nursing school when they found out she'd secretly married. Babe hated the way Rose seemed so happy to erase the family story. She would grab me by the arm as she talked, her hand dry and powdery against my skin, and ask me why her sister told so many fibs. But perhaps Rose didn't lie so much as make herself into a fiction she came to believe, becoming herself a living version of the alabaster city.

Rose remembered Chicago's hazy spires, the two-digit address on the building where she'd worked on Michigan Avenue. The numerals floated before her like voices from a heavenly metropolis that now whispered to her late at night, voices she whispered back to, saying, I'm ready, anytime now, whatever your plan is for me, the management of her celestial city having transferred seamlessly from Mayor Daley to God.

Inset of a Far Better City

In AA the geographical solution is when we move to a new place in order to make ourselves over, and thus avoid confronting the reasons we needed an overhaul in the first place. Could it be that I'm drinking too much? Is it a problem that I smoke pot alone every night until I fall asleep with the pipe still glowing? Or is the place where I live the trouble? We might wish to get conscious, but the shimmer of an easier, softer city distracts.

When I left Illinois it was because I thought my geography was killing me. I thought location—not lack of will, not pot-and-vodka-tonic-induced torpor—was keeping me from moving forward into my own life. Oh, my aching geography. After I'd dropped out of the University of Illinois, I thought I could save enough money to move back up to the city. But I didn't make it. I drank too much, both with friends and at work, so much in fact that some winter nights, walking home alone after waiting tables at a motor inn dining room—where I stole wine from the house spigots and begged cocktails from the lounge bartender—I fell into snowdrifts, laughing, honestly believing it was hilarious, the way I was living.

Once I sat on the curb of a leafy Urbana street with a bottle of blackberry brandy, drinking at 8 a.m. My then boyfriend, Leonard, had just moved that morning, packing all his books and tools and beer into a vw wagon, driving away toward his own geographical solution, in Minnesota, leaving me free to do whatever I wanted. I was ambivalent about our relationship, yet still felt unmoored. What I wanted, first off, was to drink, which I did, right there on the street. *If anyone sees me out here they'll think I'm an alkie*, I thought. And I laughed again.

I had a map of the world then, pinned to the wall in my studio apartment. Along the bottom I'd written HEJIRA, the title of my favorite album, by Joni Mitchell, where Joni herself appears in the cover art, standing in a black beret and matching cape on a smoky road, an empty highway superimposed over her torso. Under HEJIRA I wrote, in black magic marker, one of its definitions, a translation from the original Arabic: *Any trip or journey to a far better place*. I put pins in cities—New York, Hong Kong, London—that seemed to me much better than Urbana. If the Emerald City of Oz had appeared on my map, I would have pinned it too. I'd never been near any of those places, but liked to imagine myself in that black beret, smoking, stopping traffic, a flask of brandy in my stocking. But really I had little idea where, or how, to live.

Perhaps my geography *was* killing me. In the history of cities, the steeple and the skyscraper have always been confused. Both are temples that feed our longing. Both are bridges to sanctuary beyond the reach of the human body. They are another kind of geographical solution. In the years since then I've been to most of the cities on my old map, and still when I stand staring up at a skyscraper, what I feel is akin to a crush on a movie star. It's too easy to forget that temples are not gods, feelings not necessities. What cathedrals, oversize Ferris wheels, the tallest buildings ask us to do is to feel small and hungry in the light of dismissive wonder, to feel full of want, pulled to possess what might feed that want.

Inset of the Steel Mill City

Great-Grandma Kata, long before she was Gram Rose's mother-in-law, not yet eighteen, not yet emigrated, her hair loose around her ears, might have gazed out from her Croatian mountain village in the direction of the sea, clenching and reclenching her fists, wanting something, wanting more, wanting out. Years later, on the other side of wanting, an American now, hair pulled tightly away from her face, she may have clenched her fists again as she glared out over Chicago's East Side port, her eyes stinging from mill smoke. Her husband, Big Petar, was off again, no doubt leaning over a rickety table and drinking with his countrymen, lost in his telling of yet another story of yearning.

Maybe Kata started out loving Chicago's well-lit wonders, the late nineteenth-century granite spires, the lace of electrical wires, the luster of new steel mills. This might have been reason enough to refuse to leave the city when her husband, who'd already dragged her from the mining towns of Michigan and Minnesota to the mills of Chicago, decided his geography would never stop killing him unless he kept pushing, continually moving onward, westward. The untried mines were always ahead. Here the machine of the city still sputtered its promises. The fire from the mills stained the lakefront orange, and the alabaster city's gleam—that phony holiness—faded fast in the stink of Big Steel.

When Big Petar and Kata had arrived in Chicago they'd joined thousands of newcomers—the Poles, the Italians, the Serbs, the Czechs, the Croats—the last rush before the new twentieth-century immigration laws shut down the exodus from southern and eastern Europe. Petar had still been a young man when they lived above the tavern on Torrence Avenue. Loose limbs on a lanky frame, an unruly mat of dirty-blond hair, a long lope of a walk, shoulders that stooped, and arms that rose up to his face when he told a joke. The long family nose. The big, excitable eyes. The creases in both his face and his clothing lined with mill dust. The smile that changed his brooding expression into an invitation to pull up a chair.

My family remembers Kata as bitter woman, pushing her husband away, but perhaps more than just Big Petar it was the never-ending wanting in both of them that pissed her off. Perhaps she'd been led to believe that in America *come, come, come* would translate to *mine, mine, mine.*

Inset of the Disillusion City

Every weekday morning of the summer I turned nineteen I took the commuter train from the southeast-side mill suburbs, up into downtown to work at a bank in the Loop, and every evening, unless I was meeting a friend, I took the train back down again. Sometimes I came up on Saturdays, getting paid overtime to reorganize the tellers' files, until the security guards shooed me out at noon.

Because it was the weekend, when the bank was closed and no customers could see me, I wore tight jeans and sleeveless blouses that I left unbuttoned too far. (When I'm alarmed by the outfits I see nineteen-year-old women wearing today—the pants that barely cover pubic hair, the visible thong—I'd do well to remember how I dressed at that age.) Even my red patent leather sandals, with a platform sole in the front and a spike heel in back, shoes that ripped up my feet when I walked west across the Loop from the train station to the bank and back, were meant to tilt me toward some edge. I wanted the city to be aware of me, but I stiffened when men yelled from street corners or sat down next to me too close in the train station waiting room. Their wanting felt too much like owning.

I never went straight home after work on Saturdays. Sometimes I boarded a city bus and rode, just to see where I would end up. I carried a 35-millimeter camera my dad had given me. I'd learned how to use it in my college classes and was working on a series: construction workers' cement-splattered boots, secretaries' neat pumps—a collage of feet, perhaps inspired by how badly my own hurt in those bloodred shoes. But I took no pictures from the bus.

One Saturday afternoon I hopped on the Lincoln Avenue line and rode it all the way to its terminus. I had no idea how far the bus would take me. Into a neighborhood I wouldn't want to be by myself? I knew the CTA bus wouldn't cross too far over city lines. My heart banged, my hands were jittery, my camera bounced between my thighs, but I kept riding, resting my head against the streaked glass as the city gradually turned over, first shops and bars and little storefront restaurants, then long stretches of brownstone walkup apartment buildings. I watched as if I was a mapmaker charged with depicting the route, internally etching intersections and street names. What I was watching for I couldn't say, but I thought I might find it from the bus.

Finally the driver pulled into a drab strip mall and stopped. The bus idled at the curb. Another bus was ahead of him, preparing to pull away and drive south, the direction from which we'd come. It was time for the driver's break. He stood up, stretched, stared at me. Was something wrong with this young string of a woman, her hair that messy curly style all the girls were wearing? She looked like she didn't eat. Her shoes were better suited for disco dancing than riding the bus, and her shirt was unbuttoned too far. He could see everything she had, not that it was much. Was she heartbroken? Drunk? Unconscious? If he yelled at her would she hear him?

End of the line is what he shouted. I looked up at him. He was correct, there was nothing for me on this bus, but what was I supposed to do about it? He repeated himself, softer this time. "End of the line, kiddo." I peered into his face and nodded, but did not get up.

The container moves. Humans combust. One terrain streams into another. Halfway to Chicago—impatient for the train to get me to the Loop before dark, in time to see those Terry Evans landscapes flanking the lakeside like detail maps set in the downtown margins— I eavesdropped on a conversation between a passenger and the conductor. The reason the train had been so late that morning, it turned out, was the onboard birth of a baby the night before, outside Minot, North Dakota. But if it's not life it's death holding up the train. The last time my mother-in-law rode Amtrak, for instance, from her home station in Wisconsin Dells to Minneapolis, her train was held up for a couple of hours after a skinny boy sitting a few rows behind her od'ed on heroin. I don't know if the midwestern mommies riding west that night surrounded the boy, if they shook him, shouting. Are you conscious? Can you hear us? At some point the conductor must have noticed. This one, he's not breathing. The train sat still in the weeds while they waited for the ambulance. If that boy made it to his far better place, he found out it wasn't located anywhere near Seattle.

Inset of the City of Mine

One night, after making love on our living-room couch, I fell asleep naked in Linnea's arms. When I opened my eyes again she was watching me. I whispered, *What do you see?*

Mine, mine, mine, she whispered back. Possession, she was trying to tell me, is not always a matter of empire. Some possess land, but others take conscious possession of their senses. I take myself to Linnea, awake, and thus I take Linnea, by which I mean I take her desire to hold what I wish to give. What I wish to give is bound to what I once lost, or had taken, when I was a young woman too drunk to choose what I gave, lacking the wherewithal to accept or reject

FIG. 5. *Thornton Quary, Thornton, Cook County, September 17, 2003* by Terry Evans. South Side limestone out of which the city was made.

how lovers, or even strangers, fucked me. The better light comes, as we say in AA, of neither regretting nor denying history.

There is a retaking that comes of reseeing. To reenter the city with full possession of the senses is to be able to see not just what I want, not just what I remember, but also what is, now and always, really there. That girl in the Saint Paul train station, maybe she was in trouble, maybe she was just having a bad day, but the girl I keep looking for, the girl who was me, she is always present, always unconscious, then conscious again.

One of Terry Evans's photographs frames a limestone quarry in the near south suburbs, close to the house where I lived when I was that girl, still in high school. While sitting in our kitchen, my family occasionally heard the excavation blasts, almost loud enough to rattle the plates in our cabinets. This was some of the limestone out of which the downtown skyline was made. The Thornton Quarry I remember is a grind of trucks and shovels, steel against stone, but from the air, in Evans's photographs, the scarred stone walls become also sculpted sand, the truck road descending to the canyon bottom remade as a delicate spiral.

My *Empire Builder* did finally lurch into this truck-and-shovel Chicago, through the backyards of the northern suburbs, past the junkyards and warehouses at the edge and into the hum of the center itself. If this were a hundred-plus years ago and I were on one of the trains headed to the world's fair, I might be the woman thinking: *I am insignificant.* By this I would have meant not so much small as lacking comprehension, taking up space yet unworthy of my own attentions. Which is the way I felt more than a century later, in the train depot just west of the river, the second Union Station, rebuilt on this same spot in 1925, then refurbished in the 1980s into a maze of escalators and closed-in waiting rooms. I came up the escalator toward the doors and bumped into bodies moving in every direction, all busy with purposes that didn't concern me.

The purposes of jostling strangers don't concern our lady fairgoer either. She is so overwhelmed she fears she might faint in the station center, where the floor stinks of furniture wax and dust and the muddy heels of farmers' boots. No one will see her if she falls. No one will shout—Dearie, Missy, can you hear me? But she doesn't faint, nor does she call out or even sit on a polished wood bench. She circles the perimeter, holding tight to the handle of her valise, watching for the way to Congress Street. She hasn't awoken yet, but hold on, she will.

I opened the station door with my back, rolled my luggage out onto the same Congress Street. I would be here, this time, for just three days. What did I want from my Chicago, illusory or real, from

Linnea, from my marriage, from my adult life waiting patiently back in Minneapolis? I looked ahead, at the gray Chicago River, then up at the foggy glass and granite boxes of downtown, some city struggling to be tall in me.

Later still I walked south to the cusp of Buckingham Fountain, the same three tiers of spouting water set between Michigan Avenue and the lake that I'd watched from behind a car window when I was a girl, without ever getting so close. Simple awareness can locate, mere recognition that the wide-awake body is a map of obtainable and un-obtainable wants. That a woman standing near the spray of a fountain is bound to get wet. That a plain prickle of water beading across the skin on a sunny afternoon, the refracted bend of the skyline caught in its sphere, creates a deliverable shimmer.

The alabaster city is the real city's map of the perfect body we will never be.

MAP 2

Alabaster City's Gleam
A body map of Chicago, with insets

Inset of Blond Bodies

My mother is blond the day I am born. This is 1959, an early morning in late April, the same day the *Chicago Sun-Times* runs a photo-essay called "Chicago in Silhouette." The newspaper photographs are geometries of bridge girders, horizons of smoky obelisks—smokestacks lined up across the gray landscape, upright like matchsticks with their fires snuffed out. The shadowy photos expose the struts and stacks of the city's bones. Outside rain-streaked hospital windows the real city rises in relief against a newsprint sky as Mom grimaces, birthing her first child, her only daughter. My mother is blond, or I imagine her so, harsh lights revealing brunette roots.

There might be forceps and there must be drugs, a sharp needle in the thigh, my mother lost in a numb cloud out of which I emerge into the last gasp of the American 1950s, naturally blond and dollish. Later on my dad will balance me on his shoulder the way I will see him do, thirty-five years later, with my brother's baby daughter Adria. I'll smile from my Daddy-top view, peering over the horizon's curve, beyond the dingy fingers of the factory stacks, trying to reach over the South Side mills and freeways and train tracks, to where the downtown skyscrapers turn on all their lights for my benefit.

Look at these, will you? I say to Linnea at home in Minneapolis on my forty-fifth birthday, a book of gray photographs of Chicago bridges and factories open on my lap. The photos were taken by a *Sun-Times* staff photographer, Howard Lyon, a studious-looking fellow in round spectacles pictured in the front pages of a book of Chicago news photos. The staff photographers are lined up like a graduating class, holding big, old-timey cameras, the kind that used 4x5 negatives, standard issue in 1959, with hot flashbulbs that had to be replaced by hand after every shot. Howard is just one of eleven dapper white guys in neckties and fedoras, wool overcoats hanging down past their knees, pockets full of new and spent bulbs. They look like the cast of a 1950s detective flick, one of those dark-lit films full of shadows and angles, set in the wet light of the city at night.

Did Howard Lyon's pals call him Howie, as in Howie, can you take get the night beat this week? Howie's photos capture the city I carry under my skin. His pictures are industrial Chicago, the gray girders and beams that hold up the beauty queen skyline. I imagine Howie up all night, shooting the noir version of a city busy birthing a new batch of my generation, kids who would come of age just after all the rock stars started dying of overdoses, just before all the gay men started getting sick with a mysterious new disease, a generation big on longing and short on memory, kids like me who rose up out of this gray factory and warehouse plain longing for a life in living color and perhaps a little too easily mesmerized.

When my niece Adria was ten I told her about the word *mesmerize*. She had only visited the family homeland of Chicago, the way the children of my generation visit the old neighborhoods close to the mills or the older cities of Eastern Europe, second- or third-generation returnees rather than residents. Adria tells me she likes the sounds of words, which may be true or may just be the best way she knows to get her auntie's undivided attention. She's a smart kid, and her methods work.

What does this mean, she asked, pointing, in a story I'd written for her, to the long train of a word she hadn't seen before.

It means when you can't stop looking at something that you really love, or really hate, or love and hate at the same time, I told her. It means something is so beautiful or unusual or bright that it sort of hypnotizes you, and you just can't stop looking. Do you know what I mean?

Adria nodded thoughtfully, and I could see her sounding out the word as she read.

Mesmerized is how I feel when I look at Howie's pictures, even though I see the city now from a distance, as an expatriate, in ways I couldn't if it were still an everyday thing for me to stand on Michigan Avenue, looking up, which means it may not be the actual city at all I'm looking at, but instead some private metropolis. I stare into Howie's Chicago with love but also some kind of hate, the way I might stare at a gorgeous but indecipherable alphabet within which I recognize my own name.

Still, it's my desire to decode that alphabet that leads me to page through all kinds of picture books of the city, as it existed before I was born. I love photographs of State Street as it would have looked to Great-grandma Kata, though from the stories I've heard she would never have worn her pressed and parted black hair piled and poofed above her forehead—like the elegant lady shoppers in the photographs—and would probably have been too poor and dirty, the stains of the mines and the mills too visible on her face, hands, clothes to join the white-hatted ladies for tea in Marshall Field's Walnut Room, the same seemingly ceilingless space at the center of the State Street store where my best friend's mother took us to lunch when we were girls.

Inset of Hidden Bodies

Guinevere's mom loved Marshall Field's and shopped there so much my own mother, who preferred the bargains at the Dixie Square Mall Penney's, referred to Mrs. Pulicki as rich, in the way people say that word, small and bitter between the tongue and the teeth, when they assume another family in the neighborhood has more than they do, even if their wealth is only show. Mrs. Pulicki didn't work. Her husband, Guinevere's father, was a salesman—I never knew of what—the kind of guy who worked all day in his basement home office, paid on commission, who seemed to always have a telephone receiver in his hand and could *talk your ear off* if you gave him a minute. Mrs. Pulicki talked all day too. She spent her mornings in a pale cotton housedress, tossing out seeds and chatting to the backyard birds. It used to drive Guinevere nuts when we were teenagers, the way her mother loved those birds.

We were too young to understand that there's no accounting for what some people love. God knows Mrs. Pulicki would never understand why we were so enthralled with the lyrics to the Derek and the Dominos album Guinevere stole from her brother's room, or why we were so intrigued by the ads promising the benefits of those ugly flat-toed Earth Shoes, no matter how many times we explained that wearing them was *exactly* like walking in bare feet down a sand beach. We were mesmerized by progress. Our parents would never understand.

Mrs. Pulicki is the last woman I remember wearing one of those housedresses that would go out of fashion with the advent of the sweat suit. This soon-to-come change in wifely fashion was ironic in the case of my family, because a sweat suit was exactly what my mother wore to work, in her case function coming long before fashion. Mom left the house by 6 a.m. in order to get to school in time to teach field hockey in early-bird gym class. Her hair was ratted. Her sweat suit was polyester, with a zipper up the jacket front and a white stripe down the outer leg.

In my mom's eyes women who wore housedresses and fed the birds were rich, their daughters, especially Guinevere, who she once spotted wearing a muff, were spoiled princesses, and anyone who lived in yellow brick houses across from the commuter train station instead of in a brown brick bungalow across the alley from sooty Halsted Avenue was some kind of Far South Side gentry. Marshall Field's, unless they were having a sale, was not our store the way it was Mrs. Pulicki's. My mother was not interested in all that show; we remained loyal to Penney's until the 1970s, when John Belushi and Dan Akroyd smashed up dead old Dixie Square during the filming of the first *Blues Brothers* movie, the same film that begins with the slow pan of my old South Side smokestack plain.

The difference between the show and the truth is like the difference between the map and the terrain, which in our family meant the difference between a working mother's Penney's and an out-to-lunching mother's Field's, between real stores where we still really shopped and a dead mall that's torn up for the movies, between a skyscraper city and a smokestack city. That's what I see in the old pictures of Chicago, the way the bones of the city are hidden by bright lights, the way both my family and Guinevere's had stories that didn't show.

Inset of Spectacular Bodies

Take Marshall Field's Walnut Room, completed to coincide with the Columbian Exposition. At Christmastime at Field's the tables of the Walnut Room circled a seven-story Christmas tree. My little Polish grandmother used to take me to see that tree, but we viewed it only from the outside looking in. We took the elevator, the old kind with a metal gate and an operator, up to the higher levels, and stared down at white coffee cups and saucers, and the waitresses in plain black dresses and square white shoes, and the heads of all the people sipping soup or choosing a bread stick. The Walnut Room was swaddled and silent, embraced on all sides by imported-wood walls and lit from above by an invisible sky, set in the cradle of an interior courtyard, an inaccessible sanctum hollowed out of the center of the store of dreams. Peering in from the outside we could see the tree sparkling as if sprinkled with selections from the first-floor jewelry counter.

My mother's mother, Little Grandma, was short; by sixth grade I was bending over to speak to her. She wore black shoe boots and a cloth coat with a fake fur collar and a gauzy babushka over her wig. She took the bus downtown nearly every day, either to shop for something or to return something she'd bought the day before. Shopping and returning was what she did, always in search of the one right thing that was never right once she got it home to the apartment, a brownstone walk-up a block from the old projects, where her husband, my grandfather, was drinking and yelling again.

Marshall Field's was just for looking. If Grandma needed to buy something Wieboldt's or Goldblatt's still had stores on State Street, and even closer, in the South Side neighborhood of Roseland, was Gately's Peoples Store where there was always something on sale. We went to Field's only at Christmas, to see the street-level window decorations and to see the tree, from above and through glass. Little Grandma said to me, They put that tree up every year, see? I nodded and stared.

Not everyone sees Chicago as Howie saw it, as a city with a newsprint sky. As with most cities, the description depends on which side of the city one stands. From the north the city is positively blue, silver blue, like the color of light refracting off the belly of an airplane. From the condo where Linnea's sister lived until her babies started school, on the eighth story of a nineteenth-century building, you can look down on both the big blue lake and the long green park. This is Lincoln Park, the wide grassy finger with a zoo at the center, set between the brick and stone three-story flats and Lake Shore Drive, once the grandest boulevard in Chicago, where in the early twentieth century the rich men of Theodore Dreiser novels impressed shop girls with carriage rides and in 1871 surviving citizens of the first wooden version of the city huddled, their ripped clothing stinking of smoke, watching the Great Chicago Fire burn their world to the ground. In both cases the park held people stuck in the act of bargaining, forced to choose between their belief in the way things were supposed to be and the way things really were.

The question of how to view Chicago—as a gray city, as a glistening city—dates back over one hundred years before my sister-in-law married a downtown lawyer who worked his way up to a luxury view, over seventy years before I noticed a South Side smokestack for the first time, sixty-some years before my father picked up my mother at the Trumbull Park projects behind Wisconsin Steel to take her out on a date, fifteen years before my grandfather, age three, had his first look at America while holding my great-grandmother's hand on the deck of a transatlantic steamer. Columnists describing the 1893 world's fair city dubbed the rest of the metropolis, the actual Chicago, the Gray City, because of both its color and its character in contrast to the bright white exposition.

The alabaster city was actually white, made out of a temporary building material called staff—plaster, cement, and, of all things, hemp. The pothead teenager part of my brain can't stop thinking that the architects must have meant for the very composition of the city to make its visitors high. If the White City was the real city's dream of itself, the Gray City, just beyond the borders of the alabaster city, beyond even the fair's own grimy Midway with its world-record Ferris wheel and hootchy-kootchy dancing girls, was that real city. Fairgoers rented hotel rooms for anywhere from 75 cents to $4 a night, sampled local taverns, shopped in State Street department stores, bought the services of prostitutes, or, if they had missionary inclinations, saved a few corroded souls. The White City was everything the Gray City was not, the bleached-blond version of the real. The industrialists who financed the fair said the White City was the Gray City's future, and they did everything they could to keep the White City white, even forbidding the burning of coal within the fairgrounds to make certain no soot would mar the pearly surface.

Some historians even say that the exposition city embodied the notion of the ideal white American body, stripped of all its messy pelvic thrusts and hootchy-koo lusts, bodily desire contained safely in the make-believe native villages and out-of-context hip-switching Middle Eastern dance halls of the Midway. According to the unmitigated racist logic of the time, non-Western people of the world had too much body, while the Europeans and second- and third-generation European Americans had none at all, and the dirty illiterate immigrants flooding into America from eastern and southern Europe were caught somewhere in between. Columbia's bare breasts were not the same sort that drove men wild in the dance halls; her exposed nipples signified not so much sex as conquest.

Meanwhile, up the street from the Midway, the alabaster city turned heads like a blond movie star, striking the people dumb with the notion that progress—not the factory soot and stink, but something as clean and unbodied as an idea—could be so blond and beautiful we would forget that this was the end of the nineteenth century, the thick of the Industrial Revolution. In this new and supposedly progressive America children still worked in the factories. Poor women bore baby after baby, managing to keep only some of them alive. Immigrants lost limbs in the Chicago stockyards or died in the mills and mines. A few workers even lost their lives in the hellish days getting the White City ready to open.

Even now in Minnesota I skim the Chicago papers nearly every day on the Internet. My habits have been a lot like the habits of my parents, who for years now have watched the WGN Chicago News on cable in their Florida A-frame, sitting diagonally from one another on their brown leather pillow-top sofa and matching easy chair, my mother's hair dyed blond again since she retired. She caught up on the daily soap opera of Chicago, curled up next to, first, her brindle boxer Tosca, named after a character in one of my dad's favorite operas, and later her coppery girl, another boxer named Diva. Did they really need to know—as Mom drank a glass of red wine and Dad sipped his evening martini—about another South Side murder or that a guy was killed when he tried to run across the Dan Ryan Expressway? Did I really care that Marshall Field's was bought out by Macy's or that the recent Mayor Daley, son of the Mayor Daley of my childhood, had been once again swatting off charges of corruption? The only home I've ever owned is in south Minneapolis, and my current city councilman, the former lover of a man Linnea and I have known since we were still university students, is a guy I know well enough to chat with while waiting in line at the bank. Still, for most of the years I've lived in Minneapolis I've known more about what was going on in Chicago.

One of the big stories in the Chicago papers one spring was about some people in a boat on the Chicago River in the Loop. As they chugged under a bridge they suffered a shower of fresh shit let loose from the holding tank of a famous rock band's tour bus. What were all those people doing lounging around in an open-air boat on a sunny weekday afternoon? Getting mesmerized by buildings, of course. They were on one of the six daily cruises sponsored by the Chicago Architecture Foundation. Up they gazed from their cupped seats just above the water, staring at the wondrous creations of human progress, as people have been staring at buildings in Chicago ever since they came to see the alabaster city. The people in that twenty-first-century tour boat gazed up into the girders and glass of the city as if into the nave of a cathedral, but instead of communion they were blessed with a stream of shit in the face, one of those unhappy meetings of progress and egress, the city of dreams colliding with the real city of the body.

I've taken that boat ride twice myself, once with my dad and another time grinning and holding hands furtively with Linnea, beaming because this was something I'd always wanted to do with her. Chicago didn't belong to Linnea's family the way it did mine. She went to high school in a suburb so far north it might as well be Milwaukee. She has Swedes on her father's side who visited Chicago, and one great-uncle who'd lived there long ago, but most settled on the upper peninsula of Michigan, and the Italians on her mom's side live as far away as south Jersey. While my father would spend his down time driving out of his way to make sure we got a good look at the skyline, Linnea's father relaxed with his kids as far away from the city as possible, in a rustic cabin in the far north, at a little lake at the end of a dirt road.

So I couldn't wait to take Linnea into the center of my favorite place, describing to her my lifelong dream of living in one of those apartments within the downtown skyline, curved windows looking out over both the South Side smoke and Lake Michigan.

Linnea and I stared up at the granite and limestone angles and sheer cliffs of glass while the docent told us, through a scratchy speaker, about architectural moods that shifted with the decades. We held hands sneakily, because this was not my mirage but actual Chicago, a city I fear as much as love. The city has changed utterly since my childhood—rainbow flags flapping from the lampposts of Boystown, openly queer library archives, suburban LGBT nightclubs, out-and-proud couples holding hands as they walk the lakefront—but part of me still expects, when I'm in Chicago, to end up like those people on that other tour boat, with a face-full.

Inset of Bodies So Real

In 1951 the Chicago writer Nelson Algren compared Chicago to a woman. *Like loving a woman with a broken nose, you may well find lovelier lovelies. But never a lovely so real.* This goes along with my thinking, which is that if the great wide region of Chicago were the figure of a woman she would probably not be made of alabaster. In truth Miss Lady of Chicago would likely not have white skin at all, at least not all the time. She could be one of the fabulous black girls riding the downtown train in the 1960s who modeled their look on Diana Ross, from neighborhoods either north or west of where I lived, their fabulous girl-group hair straightened and sometimes even bleached, piled another head high over their foreheads, fingernails nearly as long as fingers themselves, girls who in some cases may not always have been biological girls, although I wouldn't have noticed then.

Or she would be one of the tough girls from the other side of the expressway with Mexican dads and Polish moms, part of the crowd who sat huddled along the far wall in my high school history class, my speechless admiration of their embroidered denim jackets and jeans with back pockets faded in the shape of a pack of cigarettes, one of my earliest traceable lesbian moments, even though it was their brothers I dated.

Or she might be one of my party friends, white girls with noticeably Slavic last names, our actual skin color closer to olive than alabaster, whose parents, like mine, all came from the old steel mill neighborhoods on the East Side—Mick-e Musicki (short for Michelle, the hyphen her own reinvention), who always got high before first period, or Wendy Wosinski, who was smart enough to get a scholarship to college but instead got married at nineteen, telling me lesbians and gays were okay, sure, but she would never want any around her kids.

Or she might be one of the females of my family—the slightly grimy descendants of the southern and eastern European immigrant ships—perhaps Little Grandma in her brown wig and big purse full of the crackers and sugar packets nabbed after our lunch in the Gately's Peoples Store restaurant. Or Gram Rose in her round-toed pumps and smooth hosiery. Or Mrs. Pulicki keeping city birds happy in her backyard garden, or my mother driving to work in her sweat suit with a whistle around her neck and a clipboard with the day's attendance sheets sitting next to her in the passenger seat, or Guinevere and I, still just thirteen, walking the streets of our mill suburb late at night, telling each set of parents we were at the other's house, wearing low-slung jeans and glow-in-the-dark rock band T-shirts, descending into the dim light of basement rec rooms where we learned to smoke pot without visibly freaking out.

I come up with this notion of Chicago as a woman because Chicago feels to me like a body I left behind and because of the way nations and industries and revolutions are so often depicted as big-boned gals, charging some frontier, pale and underdressed, alabaster breasts shimmering, intended to mesmerize but never getting mesmerized themselves.

Take our Miss Columbia, gem of the ocean, poster girl of Chicago's Big American Fair, where she takes the form of what was then the largest electric fountain in the world. This Columbia rides on the tiptop of a ship's mast, naked from the waist up. She's a tad gaudy at night but also a crowd pleaser when illumined like a stripper by colored spotlights. The people stare at her and, according to reports, feel heat rising in their chests, cannot immediately look away.

I need another lady to be my guiding body. Not Columbia. Someone more familiar. Little Grandma riding the CTA bus downtown with a shopping bag balanced on her knees. Gram Rose, her hair twisted into a snowy white topknot, sitting still in her powder blue car, stuck in rush-hour traffic again on the Dan Ryan. My mother in her sensible beehive, cut close around her ears. Me at sixteen, in worn jeans with ripped-out knees, crouched behind the garage, goose-pimpled in the damp air, smoking a fat and poorly rolled joint, trying my best to get good and mesmerized.

I haven't told young Adria about the dangers of getting too mesmerized. Maybe I should. Any of the hundreds of stories I've heard in two decades of AA would do. But her enthusiasms are part of what I love about my niece. When she reads her own poems to me she frowns a little, and she brushes her blond-tipped hair off her shoulders. She reads slowly, as if she's tasting each word before she lets it go. I don't want to interrupt with confusing disclaimers and warnings.

When Adria was still little, before she started school, Linnea and I took her to a Gilbert and Sullivan opera, something with fluffy wedding-cake costumes and soldiers bedazzled by the wink of a lady. I don't remember much of the plot, but I do recall the orange-reds and yellows of the costumes, and I remember Adria standing—except for a couple of interruptions when she needed an adult to run her to the bathroom—the whole time, her little face smooth and rapt, her tongue sometimes sticking out of the corner of her mouth, held by the rippling costumes and the rising pitch of the sopranos, and what else? The slamming of doors? The discharge of pistols? The high pitch and tumble of operatic laughter? I tried to imagine how it looked through her eyes. Was it like her dollies had come alive? Like a cartoon starring real people? I knew then that if she'd let me I would be one of the grown-ups in charge of her mesmerization. You're their two Auntie Mames, my gay boyfriends love to say, when we tell them stories about entertaining our nieces and nephews. Yes. Okay. I do want that job.

But should I tell her too about the things that will bore her, or worse, about the way you can be sitting outside getting high behind your parents' garage, grooving on the pale dots of stars and the slow drip of red light from a passing plane and loving the wail of a freight train that whistles like a mechanical bird until suddenly it all turns inside out and you're sure the plane is falling, that train is coming right at you, and those stars aren't stars at all but holes in the fabric of night, so old and worn away that they are ripping open? Auntie Mame, bewitching as she was with her sequined gowns and long cigarettes, did turn out to be a disappointment. But who wants to give bad news to a kid?

Inset of History's Body

Let's say I had been among the masses drawn to the alabaster city in 1893, no random fairgoer this time but instead a writer for the paper, the weekly gazette of a little copper-mining city in the upper peninsula of Michigan. So I traveled to the fair to report, like Miss Marian Shaw of the *Fargo Argus*, who wrote of the new wonder of electricity, equal, she described, to 194 million candle flames.

If this version of me took the train down to the city, I'd have worn my best starched professional blouse, my heavy skirt hanging neat to my ankles, my dark blond hair in a marshmallow puff over my long forehead, my hair, of course, not bleached blond.

If I'd scribbled on the back of the postcard to the young niece who'd wanted to come with me I might have written:

The city is made of white columns, white doorways bent as an acrobat's back. Honey, have you ever seen an acrobat? I wish you were here with me to see this place; white fountains erupt like sudden flower stems and the statues are beautiful ladies of art and industry who ride on the barge of state, breaking the mirror of the lagoon with the flat backs of marble oars while Columbia, Miss America herself, rides overhead, the wind in her hair.

And if I were anything like the woman I am now, I would have stopped writing then, worried at how much to reveal to the child. I would have noticed not just the figure of the alabaster lady but also her exposed nipples, open to the brisk wind of a choppy lagoon, and I would have felt bothered under my own blouse and would've insisted on knowing why things displayed at this fair were not entirely what they seemed.

There were good reasons a girl like me wanted out of the 1970s south mill suburbs. The mill fields between where we lived and the skyline promise of downtown contained one of the highest concentrations of dumps and landfills in America. The steel mills themselves were getting ready to shut down, and so the economy of the region was tanking. Now, all these years later, I know lesbians who live openly down there, but back then the gay girls in those parts kept quiet.

But that doesn't quite explain it. I didn't move away planning to turn out gay. Desire is not always so specific. Perhaps, when it comes to wanting, I'm not all that different from Mrs. Pulicki, who I see now did not take us to lunch at Marshall Field's because she was rich, as my mother thought, but because she wanted to be, and perhaps even felt like she was in that long moment between the last nibble of chicken pot pie and the first whiff of cold Frango mint. *Never a lovely so real*, wrote Algren, and I think he meant not the dirty or the clean but the less certain space of the transitory zone in between.

Inset of Miss Body of Chicago

The famous Chicago skyline pictured on architectural posters and refrigerator magnets is shot from somewhere out on Lake Michigan. But hardly anyone actually gets to see the city from that clean vantage point. To get downtown when I was a child, by car or train or bus, we had to ride through the steel mill stink, past the block-long window-less plant buildings, around the industrial lots fringed with remnants of prairie grass. *Whatta dump*, slurs Miss Lady of Chicago, a little drunk from the mill fumes, staggering over the junkyards along the Calumet Expressway. But this lady's bare toe is not so much floating as dragging across the trash-spattered shores of the Calumet River.

She travels over a charcoal landscape of colorless grain elevators, tall as office towers and wide as aircraft carriers, dirty yellow paint-refinery lights brightened by the occasional burst of orange flame from the open mouth of a factory stack, and acres upon acres of garbage dumps and landfills, punctuated here and there by a finger or two of sickly trees. Behind her the steel mills are rusting and the trains are stacked like piles of slag. Cars flee her dirty toes and the commuter trains whine as they rush out of her way. Up ahead the city housing project towers stare with the blank eyes of career drunks. Miss Lady of Chicago is headed downtown, and she's made some progress, but she's coughing up a cloud of mill fumes and freeway dust. She's tired, her head is hanging, and she's taken off her wig, clutching the blond mop in her hands as if she's afraid someone will try to snatch it away. The skyline is a beacon, but it might also be a mirage. I'm not sure she's going to make it all the way to the fair.

Despite everything that can go wrong—the bad things I want to warn Adria about—I don't think I could live without staring up into some kind of skyline. And things do go wrong. Let's say I notice the Marshall Field's Christmas tree is gaudy and find out that they don't make a great espresso in the Walnut Room. Or I discover the ways most cities stink on summer afternoons before the garbage is picked up, or I'm scared to death when the first woman I think is the love of my life gets really mad at me, especially when I know the whole trouble is my own damn fault. Or maybe I've gotten hooked on shoplifting, even boast of how good I am at it, until I get caught by an undercover store dick and am dragged into a backroom where they make me empty out my bag and sign a police report. Or I finally figure out booze and pot are as likely to make me sick and paranoid as anything else, but then realize that even though I've quit cold turkey I have nightly dreams about slipping into coat closets to chug white wine. When I start tabulating it's easy to decide that life is a long dump of shit in the face.

Still, if we were never let down, what would there be to get excited about? I get it why all those people came to the fair and stared. *They put that tree up every year, see?*

Inset of the Body of Hope

While Guinevere's mother was lost in the chirping of her backyard birds, Mr. Pulicki was in sheer physical pain, in his back, probably related to all the hours sitting in a desk chair, talking fast into the phone, in the years before ergonomics. His back got so bad it eventually paralyzed him, but before that time he always walked with an awkward limp. As a girl I noticed his walk without thinking about it. Mr. Pulicki seemed huge and square to me, especially compared to my own slim and athletic parents, who, due to my mother's gym training, were fitness freaks long before it was in fashion. It wasn't until we were adults that Guinevere explained that her father was in constant, chronic agony. As kids we just never talked about what it meant to hurt all the time.

But for a while, in the early 1970s, Mr. Pulicki got better. He traveled to a South Sea island for his appointments with one of those faith healers, the kind that could take people's internal organs out of their bodies and slap them back in again without ever making an incision. Guinevere showed me the pictures. Could it be real? There was her dad, his pale blocky body bared on the operating table, his exposed toes pointing up, and an efficient-looking man in a white doctor's coat standing beside the metal table, frowning intently, holding Mr. Pulicki's jellied organs in his outstretched palm. Mr. Pulicki was a believer. He came home all jazzed up, smiling and talking, talking and smiling. Finally a life lived without a knife in his back.

It wasn't real, of course. He did end up just as paralyzed, still on the phone, Guinevere tells me, twenty-five years later, selling things, until right before he died, even when he couldn't move any part of his body from the neck down. Faith healing was just the scam du jour. They took Mr. Pulicki's money, quite a lot of it, I understand, but they didn't heal him, and for that they were criminals. And yet for a time they made him believe he could be healed. Would it have been better for him to avoid that detour and have traveled directly from pain to paralysis? If we don't ever believe we're getting close to the city of 194 million candles, what then is the point of the journey?

Inset of the Body of Light

I'm in the backseat of our blue station wagon, next to my two crew-cutted brothers. My dad drives with one elbow out the driver's side window. This might be the year he smokes an occasional cigarette, which my mother hates. If so, he blows smoke out the window as we drive. It might also be the year he grows a moustache, thick on his upper lip, speckled with the white whiskers that eventually, had he kept it, would have matched the color of his hair.

My father could not turn away from the lit-up city. It was my mother who taught me to recognize Howie's gray photos of the city in silhouette, the way she crinkled her nose and turned away from the car window whenever we passed the sulfur stink of a steel mill. But it was Dad who taught me the religion of looking up, coached us on how to be conscious always of where we were, driving the long way home no matter how my mother complained.

That day in the station wagon Mom is a brunette. She will stay that way for the rest of my childhood, her hair, supported by a hair piece, ratted into a beauty parlor bouffant tall as a brownstone apartment, a style she will keep until perms come into fashion. Meanwhile my dad slows down as we merge into the traffic on Lake Shore Drive, gesturing with his chin, making sure we notice the sun setting behind the skyline. Light shimmies from the city's belly, catches the sequins of Miss Lady of Chicago's cocktail dress, flickers over the seats of the car, and covers our forearms and bare legs with bright spangles. I'm not sure my brothers are looking. It might just be my father and I, each of us private in our silence, quietly getting a little bit mesmerized.

See, see, I say to Linnea, holding the *Sun-Times* book in my lap, open to Howie's photos. I need her to understand. Linnea nods and peers, even though I haven't even given her a chance to change out of the nice tailored men's suit she wears to work. All she needs is a brimmed hat with a tiny copper feather and she'd look right at home on the liquid streets of Howie's 1950s Chicago, and when I tell her as much she laughs. I am surprised, I tell her, how the profile of the old Loop is so small and only occasionally peaked, nothing like the mountain range of the Chicago skyline today. Even little Minneapolis has a much more impressive skyline in 2005 than Chicago did in 1959.

But now I am pointing to Howie's shots of seven smokestacks framed by a filigree of bridge girders. This is what my mother would have seen, I tell Linnea, out the window of her hospital room, the morning she had me, the image imprinted on the negative of my body, although really I have no idea if my mother had a window in her hospital room. This is why, I say, Minneapolis never feels completely right to me. Linnea nods again, even though she gets tired of my complaints that I can't live in clean blue Minnesota forever.

Yet if I had seen Howie's pics as a child I would have found them ugly. If someone had handed me a copy of the *Sun-Times* and said, Look honey, pictures from the day you were born, I would have said, Well that figures. On *my* birthday they run the ugly pictures.

Inset of Representing Bodies

If it had been me visiting in 1893 I might have written, to my niece:

> You may have heard that the views from the world's tallest Ferris wheel are breathtaking. Indeed it's true. From the tippy-top I can see the smoky checkerboard of the city grid and the endless blue reach of the lake and the ripple of farmland and what even seem to be a few patches of unplowed prairie. It changes everything to see the world from up here.

From the top of the Ferris wheel, heady with the feel of my body pushing unnaturally higher and higher into the sky, I would have seen what was invisible from the center of the fair, which is that it's

FIG. 7. *Chicago in Silhouette* by Howard Lyons, 1959.
The South Side of Chicago on the day I was born.

not the actual city but the alabaster one that's really a silhouette,
painted and propped up, not actual progress but just a picture.

Inset of My Mother's Dreams of Another Body

My mother was not really blond the day I was born. I just chose, for
a moment, to remember it that way.

But I don't entirely make up her blond-haired history. My mother
was blond for a while when she was young but let her hair grow out
to its natural brown before the day of my birth. I've seen the home
movie of the day she came home from the hospital with me, her hair
the brown bouffant I remember, held in place by a pale babushka,
holding a blanket with her firstborn bundled inside.

But I also found a snapshot from before I was born, perhaps around the time I was conceived, this one in color, my pretty mother in red plaid vacation clothes, her hair blond as Marilyn Monroe's. She's so young, about the age I was when I first moved to Minneapolis. She has just married my father. He is in the service, but it's not wartime, so he's stationed in Arizona. My mother travels down from Chicago to see him, and together they go to the Grand Canyon. The big copper hole fills up the background like a lake hungry for its missing water.

My mother stands at the edge of the rest of her life, staring back at the camera, her face clear and alight, an electric glow that makes me a little jealous. Was she ever so happy once I came along, interrupting her romance with my father? I know she will be disappointed soon. Her college major was math, PE just her minor, and because it is still the 1950s, women's careers still considered temporary, she will give up her first job, her dream position, teaching math, because she's going to have a baby. I've always known my mother's dream of herself may not have included me, at least not then, not yet. Still, like any actuality, this is a gray sort of knowledge, the kind of photograph Howie would have loved.

FIG. 8. *Bohemiae Rosa* by Christoph Vetter, 1668.

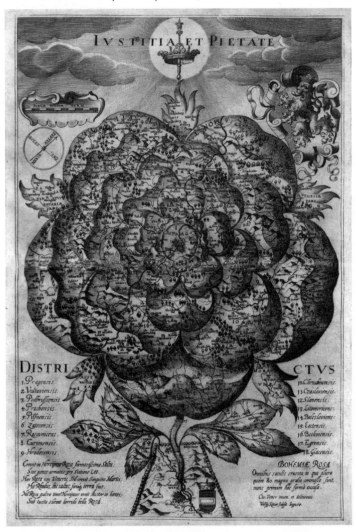

What's a Bohemian? Just a high-class Polack, my Bohemian grandmother and her sisters used to quip. Now I know: a Bohemian is also an unconventional body, a new American beauty, a rose.

MAP 3

American Doll

A map of Hong Kong imagined,
with Avenue H insets

Sometimes Gram Rose watches the Catholic channel, the slow throb of
the communion service, the camera moving in on the golden chalice,
the white moon of the host. My father's mother is nearly blind but
might be able to make out the shapes—a stemmed cup, a paper-thin
obelisk rising over the rim, a midwestern harvest moon hovering still,
even though she's lived now twenty-five years in Florida. The Vatican
choir keens through the TV speakers and she watches, sitting silently
on the TV room divan, her knees pressed neatly together. She wants that
hovering host. She wants, I think, to eat it up, though she would never
wish such an un-Catholic desire aloud, preferring we imagine her as
she's always presented herself, kneeling chastely along the altar rail,
head bent up under the chalice, swallowing the host without biting.

Inset of the Alabaster Interstate

The Chicago where I used to live fell away the year I turned twenty-
two. The gray city receded, became strange as a new city loomed. I
could feel the tips of my fingers as the blue city approached. I could
feel my hips, the space between my breasts, as if I were new.

Inset of the Gray City

My grandfather Petey thinks he remembers a little. What year was it? 1908? He was Little Petar then, not yet three, before he became Petey, an American boy. The newspapers of Chicago called his old country Yugoslavia, and that's what he calls it when he talks to the Irish or Italian boys at the mill who think the Croats, the Serbs, even the Polacks are all the same. His mother, Kata, spits when he says Yugoslavia. No such country, she says, the only words she speaks in English. He shrugs. Yugoslavia. Croatia. Who cares? He is an American boy. He will not remember the hard line of land as it looked from the boat. He will remember only the cold current in his face, his eyes fluttering closed, a fist of wind in his chest. He will kick his feet, demand his mama put him down. He will get there himself.

When Petey grows up he will work at a desk, filling out forms with spindly lines of ink, not sweating at the rim of the steel mill furnace like his brothers. He will learn the new American fox-trot and marry Rose, that beautiful American doll training to be a nurse. He will run into his American life, toes twitching, wind stinging his eyes. He will make his American babies, buy his American house on Blackstone Avenue. Then, at just forty-two, the end, a gurgle Rose hears in the night, the blood clot in his chest, bursting.

Gram Rose tells a story about taking a taxi in Hong Kong. Every time I travel down to the Gulf Coast to see her she tells me the story again. She's well into her nineties now, her short-term memory gone, but this story is the one she remembers well enough to repeat, sometimes several times a day. Each time I pretend to listen as if it were the first time. Why is this story the one she tells over and over?

I drive her down the road near the beach she has lived alongside for a quarter century, to Pineapple Willie's or Harpoon Harry's or Hammerhead Fred's, whichever beachfront bar I can find open in the off-season, as she pretends she knows where we are. I might believe she does know, except she couldn't possibly, because the place keeps changing, every month a new sand-colored condo blocking the view of the sea. Gram's snow-white hair, twisted and poofed like a 1940s movie star, looks just the same as it always has, but she's skinnier and blind now, except for hazy registers of light and familiar forms. After a lifetime of never letting on when she was scared or confused or even uncomfortable, she knows how to cover.

I don't mingle well anymore with the skinny beach children who crowd these beaches at the more popular times of year, drunk on cheap beer, their bodies oiled shiny as supermarket apples. My hair has been streaked and bobbed, my skin tattooed—an open-mouthed leopard, a Sailor Jerry rose—for longer than these beach babes have had discernible cleavage, and in this red-state zone I am a certifiable pervert because I've had more women lovers than men and have lived with Linnea for longer now than most of those kids have lived on earth. The empty beaches of off-season suit me better. I am anonymous walking the white sand under stiff wind and high sun, most of the hotels closed, marquees promising best rates for snowbirds.

The beach hangouts are all empty. It's just under sixty degrees and Gram pulls her sweater close and mumbles about the cold, but coming from midwestern winter I think the weather is perfect. Forty degrees is like *below zero* to me now, she tells me. We pass under the steel tower where the college kids will bungee-jump when this empty road turns into a carnival, come March. Gram cowers and wags her finger. There's that thing again, she mutters. I don't know what she sees. The shadow of a Chicago skyscraper? What's left of her alabaster city?

It's so unlike her to admit she doesn't know something. It unsettles me. I ask her a question, about her life before, to distract her. Gram sits back against the clean blue seat of my rental car and lapses into her usual story about the trips she took in her years as a nurse receptionist, when she was an officer in the Association of American Medical Assistants. The stories have worn a groove in her brain. Once she begins to talk she knows where she is again.

Oh I went to Hong Kong at least three times, she says. I traveled everywhere to attend my meetings, every state in the Union and also Japan, and England. But Hong Kong was my favorite.

Inset of Herself Imagined

Rose was a woman who swaggered like a starlet, not just when she stepped off the plane in Hong Kong but wherever she went. She was a lady who would give you the what for, a lady who did what she pleased. She had to. Her husband, Petey, died in his prime. She had no one to take care of her. She was perfectly capable of taking care of herself, and everyone around her, whether they wanted her to or not.

Years later, projecting my father's home movies onto a sheath of white paper taped to my living-room wall, I meet Rose in her forties, my age. Rose is already a widow, crossing the pool patio of the Stardust Motel in Arizona. How does a woman learn to walk like a movie star? I try to copy her gait, stepping across the scratched oak of my Minneapolis living room, my two curly blond dogs, Miss Dusty Springfield and Miss Rosemary Clooney, nipping at my heels, and even though I don't wear shoes I manage to twist my weak right ankle. Damn, I mumble, as the girls grin and yap. Gram Rose would have never lived with dogs.

Rose was not the type to moon in movie theaters, not the kind to perfect her positions before the bedroom mirror she shared with her younger sisters. In the 1920s her family lived on Assistance, among all the others whose names ended in *i* or *ich* or in her case *ek*, families of the grimy workmen of the East Side of Chicago, where the avenues had letters instead of names. Rose's father was worse off than some of the immigrants from Bohemia—not the *La Bohème* Bohemia but the Slavic nation—*Bohemian* just a fancy name for Polack, my relatives used to love to say. Her father was the one who'd lost his toes in a railroad work accident and then was swindled by a lawyer who'd promised to make him rich if he sued instead of accepting an easy job for life, the company's settlement offer. But whatever dough he won in the end? The lawyer took it, leaving the family waiting in line for bags of food.

Rose would never admit to standing in line for food. Rose would refuse to stand in line. She would work, but never at one of those

Bohunk jobs. She would go to nursing school, live in the clean white hospital with the other girls in training. She loved her father but was not meant to live with a family led by a man without toes. Rose was a woman who looked as if she were born in tasteful working woman's heels, a woman who expected the waters to part before her. Once those waters parted, once she'd walked safely without getting wet, it was as if there had never been water.

The Rose flickering from my living-room wall is a swaggering movie house doll, not so much a woman of the city as the alabaster city herself. Can a lady swagger? Rose strutted with the hip-centered steps I've seen since only on the runways of drag shows. Today our family blames all that Rose can't or won't remember on her age. They forget she was always the auteur of her own magnificent projection.

This is the way she walks in 1962, out of her hotel room and onto the afternoon streets of Hong Kong, while another nursing assistant, Elvira, her usual traveling companion, naps. Rose picks up her purse, not bothering to straighten her stockings because, of course, her stockings are always straight. The bell captain ushers her into a cab. Rose assumes the cab driver understands when she tells him she wishes to purchase a teapot. Why wouldn't her English be understood? The driver does not look over his shoulder at Rose, her back so straight, her face so still, as the cab pulls into the crowded street.

Inset of the Middling West

I arrived in my little city not by taxi or plane. Not by boat, not by train, not in any of the ways my relatives arrived at the middle. I pulled up in a 1973 Pinto wagon that used to belong to my uncle, the same Chicago mechanic who once owned the Blazer Linnea still drives today.

Everything I possessed was crammed into the back of that Pinto; I'd pulled up to a dumpster before leaving Illinois and tossed out anything that didn't fit. I was all long legs and long blond hair, just off a long drive out of an Illinois prairie college town. Dropout is the right word for what I was up to then, water pearling out of the mouth of a leaky faucet, hard, smooth, impenetrable, dropping out of college, out of the family's plans, another American girl hell-bent on disappointing her hardworking parents.

I traveled with a copper-colored cat used to doing as she pleased. She mewed and fussed in the back of the car all the way through Wisconsin. I had a collection of T-shirts with feminist logos decaled across the front—a clenched fist embedded into the biological symbol for woman, words that insisted we *unite* or *march on* or *take back*. I had a belief that all things ought to be more natural, more themselves, and the arrogance to think I would know the real thing when I saw it. I had experienced one tepid lesbian love affair and was watching the clock on my last affair with a man. I didn't land on the messy eastern docks of America, as my grandfather had, but in Minneapolis, Minnesota, in the liberal voting districts of a clean city with streets wider than four side-by-side Chicago semis. I didn't have to learn an entirely new language, just a new edgeless version of English—round, soft, Scandinavian-influenced talk that flinched in the presence of my dad's Slavic immigrant–laced gloom, my mother's old South Side Chicago sarcasm.

I sometimes daydream myself into the girl I might have been, the girl I'd crossed state lines to keep from becoming. I watch myself hover as if across the old Zenith TV screen, pale and suspended as the host in my grandmother's TV cathedral. The screen blips and fizzes as I adjust the picture to see the lives I've let Chicago live without me. That girl is skinny and crosses her legs when she drinks, and she blonds-up her hair, not like my actual two-toned highlights but a consistent bright bleaching. Her tresses—unlike me, she has *tresses*—gush down her back.

No. She is fat and wears the same perm she wore in 1979, and she's mom to four unruly kids who can be sweet and smart but are always in trouble at school. She lives with them in a mill suburb tract house just across the Illinois-Indiana state line. She drives a Chevy Suburban, edits a suburban shopper newspaper, avoids her asshole ex-husband, writes long letters to high school girlfriends that she never mails, and sometimes sleeps with a ponytailed teacher from the high school where her mother used to teach, the one teaching English temporarily—he loves to whisper this to her in bed—just until he finishes writing his novel.

No. She is childless, works all the time, at a job they tell her is in a *creative field*, and she lives in the near North Side of Chicago, in a high-rise with a doorman and a view of the lake. She dates downtown professional guys who live in lofts, who disappoint her, and now and then she has relations she has no words to describe with a married girl she meets in her lakefront-walking club. She likes to smoke cigs and get looped on Tanqueray tonics while she watches the sunset fall over the West Side rooftops.

When she goes south to see the family for two or three hours at a time, never longer, she doesn't drive but hails taxis to the commuter train that runs from the Loop on the old Illinois Central line. When she gets a whiff of the Calumet mills, sulfur floating north (or south, depending on which life this is), she's nostalgic for the years she was a teenager, hunched and hiding behind the garage, dreaming up ways to leave. Whichever woman I turned out not to be calls her mom once a week and they have the same fight they've had since she was fifteen, in which her mother asks her why she isn't a normal happy woman and in which she replies that a woman is only as happy as her mother teaches her to be, the same fight I was, in real life, able to stop having with my mother only after I moved away.

When I arrived in my little blue city, into the life I have ended up living, the first thing I did was drive around, marveling at the empty downtown streets, and I wondered, Is this slow season in Minneapolis? I saw that the skyway rumors were true, glass-enclosed bridges floating between the central city buildings. People might not have to go out at all before April, but this was October and the weather was balmy. In downtown Chicago at this time of year there were always Chicagoans on the streets. Where were the Minneapolitans? Downtown Minneapolis was as empty as an eggshell, the silence gray and grainy as an over-enlarged photograph. I circled the domed stadium slowly, wondered what I'd done, moving here, where the dark sports dome seemed an abandoned space saucer. The downtown lights glowed at my back like a field of fireflies, a beam here, a beam there, then gone.

Gram spends her afternoons in a warm room off her kitchen with the TV turned up loud enough for her to listen without her hearing aid. She calls this her Hang-Out Room. She taped a handwritten note to the door that reads Hang-Out Room in her uneven black marker scrawl. It might be a joke from some time when my young cousin stayed with her. It might be a map, reminding herself where she is. I'd ask, but I'm afraid she won't remember, and then I'd have to see her face freeze up again.

When Gram isn't watching the Catholic channel she's usually tuned to the all-day Fox News, the tone high and alarming—none of the companionable chuckling of the local news or even the American wise-guy cadence of CNN. On Fox the unending war is always on. Each time the anchors utter *Axis of Evil* my grandmother shakes her head.

Why does she watch this right-wing news? I ask her. My father asks her. Wasn't she a lifelong Democrat? She tells us she wants to keep up with the world. Her knee hurts, so she can't take her customary walk around the golf course to pick up the mail. It's been years now since she's driven over the bridge to Panama City to volunteer at the hospital. She feels useful now if she stays informed, if she worries her way through the day.

Gram has never been to see me in Minneapolis. She's been back to Chicago since moving to Florida, and to my cousin Dino's fancy summerhouse, up the bend from Chicago on the Michigan shore of the big lake, but she's never traveled any farther north. She swears to me that she's visited every state of the Union with her medical association yet admits she's never been to Minnesota.

Minneapolis is north, only seven hours in the car from Chicago, I tell her. I walk into the restaurant slowly, holding Gram by the elbow. Step up here, Gram, I say. Let's sit here in the sun, where it's warm. Our waitress smiles patiently as I read the menu out loud. Winter waves pound away in the background. I order for her. Chicken sandwich. Coffee. I think, How strange—to order for a woman who walked alone in Hong Kong. Minnesota is by Lake Superior, near Canada, I tell her, for the thousandth time, as we wait for the waitress to bring our drinks. I don't bother explaining that the Canadian border is five hours north of my block in the thick of Minneapolis, where lately the predominant language is either Spanish or Somali.

Too near, she mutters. Her shoulders relax in the sun. She looks right at me as if she can still see my face. Those Canadians come down here and cause all this trouble.

Canadians? I knew she disliked the Canadian snowbirds, the ones she was convinced bought up all the good food in the Winn-Dixie. But now her Canadians have taken a turn for the worse. America was a good place, she says, before those Canadians started coming down here. She doesn't say the words *hijack* or *anthrax* or *suicide bomber*, but she is shaking her head, just as she does when she listens to Fox News.

What does she see when she worries about Canadians? I doubt she knows of the complicated racial mix of twenty-first-century Canadian cities. She might not even know that some Canadians speak French. Does she imagine the lumberjacks of TV comedies—red plaid jackets and fur caps with earflaps—trundling south in military formation, a concentrated arrow of buzzing snowmobiles? Or is she confusing Canada with Afghanistan, mixing up Florida and Iraq? The fast flash of television maps might all look the same through her one fuzzy eye. Are those Taliban turbans or warm winter hats? The endless news reports repeat like prayers of the rosary. She must wonder why her family is so blasé. Why aren't we preparing? She's ready to help. She worked in the medical field. She still has all those drug samples in a bag under her bathroom sink, a little old, but still good medicine.

Inset of Her Imagined Hong Kong

Rose was never home with her second husband, not if she could help it. She went on cruises to Alaska, junkets to Japan. She went to Hong Kong. Joe-who-was-not-the-love-of-her-life would be angry if he found out what she was up to in the city overlooking Repulse Bay. Rose didn't care what that one thought. She wanted a teapot, a real one. She wanted to go to China and she would.

The cab driver turns off, away from the hotels. He is taking Rose all the way to regular China. Elvira would be angry. Elvira would call Rose's husband. How could Rose wander away like this? How could she even think of going to China on her own?

Petey would have said, Okay doll, whatever you want. Rose told the taxi driver where she wanted to go, and of course he would take her there. She could feel it as they began to get closer, communism in the air, heavy like a summer front. Elvira would worry; Rose knew that. And what if they kept her there? Captured her? But who would dare hurt an American? The taxi rolled her forward. China made her shiver, as if she were crossing through a wall of bad weather. Rose leaned forward, in order to get there quicker.

I used to try to tell Gram it was impossible. The part of Hong Kong where she stayed is an island and in 1962 still a colony of Great Britain. Since 1997 it's been part of China again, but there is still a Mainland China border, twenty-five miles north of the island. There's water to navigate, borders to pass through. In 1962 she would have needed to take a ferry and then a train. Even if she were the rich American doll she imagined herself to be, there were no car tunnels back then, no way to take a cab over the water to the mainland, unless the cabs back then could fly.

But before I did the geographical research I did wonder if Gram's story could be true. Wouldn't I want a grandmother bold enough to nod her way into Red China? I've read books about the history of the rocky island of Hong Kong, about pirates, opium sellers, and British bureaucrats. As in most colonies, a good number of the natives were segregated and poor. I squint into websites where retired navy seamen post snapshots of midcentury Hong Kong fish markets, herbal apothecaries, dumplings sizzling in streetside skillets, and narrow streets crammed shoulder-to-shoulder with Chinese shoppers—women in loose-fitting trousers and flat shoes, men in matching cotton pants and high-collar jackets or in black business suits and narrow ties. I even find a shot of a big red taxicab. It does not have wings.

Gram could have wandered no farther than out of the colonial zone of English ladies and afternoon tea, onto a narrow street where the women wore soft shoes and silk trousers and the store signs were, to Gram's eyes, a kaleidoscope of Chinese pictograms. She must have crossed a district line, a race line, and once there became mesmerized by her internal Quincy Jones movie soundtrack, the fast-paced jazz of the brisk American lady.

Inset of an American Doll

She was a doll. That's why Petey danced with her. Like the song: *Oh you big beautiful doll*. The way she walked. That swing to her hips. And ooh, she was so light on her feet. She didn't have the Old Country hanging on her back, not like those girls with their hair hidden under babushkas that his mother wanted him to notice. Whenever he saw Rose he said, Ooh, there's that beautiful doll from Avenue H.

Rose keeps Petey's photograph on her bedroom dresser, in a frame shaped like a heart. She strokes it as if she can see her dead husband's face. I ask my father, What was Petey like? Did he speak his mother's language? Did he read the Chicago papers published in both English and Croatian, the ones with advertisements for steamers that ran out of the mainland through the Great Lakes, east on the St. Lawrence Seaway, and back across the big water?

My dad shrugs and shakes his head. His father died more than fifty years ago. Dad's big sleepy eyes look cloudy to me. All he can tell me is that his father wanted to be an American.

In the few photographs I've seen of my grandfather he is slender and narrow-shouldered, strong without appearing muscular. In one black-and-white shot he stands knee-deep in beach water. This must be South Side Lake Michigan, Rainbow Beach or Calumet Park, one of those stretches of waterfront where the hard Chicago race line has since shifted, where white people hardly go anymore. This used to be my family's neighborhood. Petey wears square black swimming trunks and holds the hand of a little blond boy, my father. He looks somewhat like my father, my uncle, my boy cousins, but not as much as I expect. He has the same high bright eyes and prominent nose, yet his face stands out against the faces of the ones who came after him, not bony exactly, but looking closely I feel I can see his bones. He lacks the American roundness of his sons and grandsons. He looks more like the Balkan men I've seen in documentary photographs from the wars of the 1990s, the ones turned out of their homes at gunpoint, their eyes lit like a changing sky, their bodies stiff and set, skin loose as cloth.

My family would rather I look easier at the old photos and see our American vigor. I do see it, the stock immigration story, each generation doing a little bit better. I see all this and something else too, perhaps the weight a man carries when he pretends he has no past.

Inset of This New World

The grandchildren Little Petey will never meet are all the way American in our 1960s steel mill suburb grade schools. Rock and Roll. Bozo's Circus. I wish I were an Oscar Meyer wiener. Anything Old Country is embarrassing, like a bad smell or a spot you can't get off your glasses. Our generation loves the Brady Bunch and hippies and embroidered blue jeans and dirty bare feet. We hate the old East Side restaurants where our parents take us Sundays for accordion music and funny triangular guitars with long skinny necks, heavy food served on heavier platters, waitresses pinching our cheeks, telling us how much we look like our fathers. The relatives who *don speaka no English* are by now mostly gone, but some aunts still call their head scarves *babushkas*. So many different ways to pronounce our last name, we bow our heads until the teacher stops asking, and now even the relatives don't agree which is the right way to say it. What are you? the kids on the playground ask. We all know the answer. American, right? But everyone is also something else—Polish, Italian, Bohemian, Croatian. What's that? ask the nasty boys with last names like Cook or Smith. YU-GO-SLA-VEE-AN we say. They laugh, shrug, run away.

I am middle-aged before it occurs to me that our America was made up of things not so American. The British Beatles on our lunch boxes. Hot dogs a lot like what my mom still calls Polisausage. Bozo, a regular man's name in Croatia. Was the first American clown an immigrant? Is there a country somewhere where the buffoons are named Bob? Who could blame Grandpa Petey, Rose, me for forgetting. *Put me down. I'll get there myself.*

I leave Florida with Gram's tea set packed into my bag. After her afternoon daiquiri I drop her off at her house, just a twist and turn along the golf course from where my parents live now. I help Gram into the house and see the teapot with matching cups and tray, set atop a doily on a small round table in her dining room. I'd seen it before, but really look this time. She'd kept it nice all these years, golden and delicate and without a single chip.

I never told Gram Rose that I collect teapots, and even if I had she wouldn't have remembered. She asks me the same question every time I see her. Now who makes dinner at your house? Do you cook or does . . . and then she stumbles. Li, Lin, Len . . . All these years I've lived with Linnea, but Gram can't remember her name.

Linnea, I say, finishing for her. She nods and then asks me again. Which one of you cooks?

I always answer the same. We both cook, Gram, but different things. And Linnea is a better cook than I am. She's Italian, you know.

Oh, I didn't know that, she always says, nodding as if that explains everything, remembering perhaps when her only daughter, Cecilia, married that Italian. Gram still leans close and whispers to me, Those Italians, they're different, you know. It may be she remembers Linnea as my good friend, or it may be she sometimes confuses Linnea for a man, my American guy, one of her gentlemanly dance partners, and so thinks of me as like her daughter who married that Italian boy. Which reminds her of Dino, Cecilia's son, another one who turned out different. Dino and Danny both know how to cook, she tells me, as she has a hundred times before, but each one is better at different things. But this time she adds something new. She looks out over her dining room as if all of her grandchildren and great-grandchildren are gathered.

You and Dino are happy, she says, nodding. You did what you wanted.

I'd never really known whether or not she'd grasped the life Dino and I had come to live. Now hearing that she did, I don't know what to say to her in this spotless dining room gone shabby over the years, as the Fox News commentators bleat from the Hang-Out Room. Finally I fall back into easier terrain. Her tea set glimmers from a table in the corner. I ask, Gram, is this the teapot you bought in Hong Kong?

Oh yes, she begins. Did I ever tell you that story? This time, before she is done, the teapot is wrapped in newspaper and packed in a shopping bag. I try to refuse. What if later she forgets, then walks past and doesn't feel the cool porcelain against her knuckles? Will she insist that someone stole it? Will she feel that now, along with her knee, along with her eyes, she has lost her Hong Kong?

Inset of Her Hong Kong Imagined

Rose did not feel quite herself as she stepped into the tea shop. She wasn't herself. She had crossed a border. She saw the one she wanted right away. It was golden, with a painted firebird, its neck stretched up, out, away. Rose didn't know about the phoenix, how it rises out of nothing and creates itself. She did know that second one she married would tell her later that she was crazy; those Commies would never send her that teapot. Three weeks later, when she was home safe in Chicago, the tea set arrived, packed and wrapped so neatly, the golden pot, the matching cups, the painted tray that had crossed so many borders.

FIG. 9. *Nineteenth Precinct, First Ward Chicago* by William Stead, 1894.

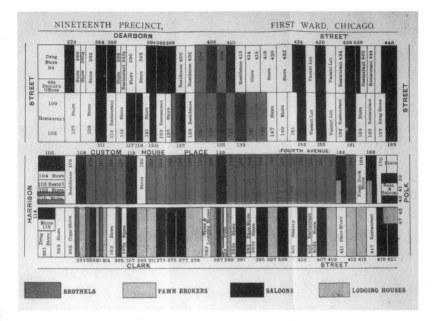

Some maps are stories about time and women's bodies.

MAP 4

Mapping the Body Back
An overlay map, with pages illegible or missing

We have no maps without the maps that came before. Lift one map of
the body and find another. Navigating back. Mapping through.

First Is the Map of Withstanding / 2007 Minneapolis

Where I like Pilates, its single or double syllabic coordinates. Core.
Pelvic. Imprint. Where I like the pictures of the former circus performer
who invented it nearly one hundred years ago—Joseph Pilates wearing
stretchy swim trunks, flexing his ropey muscles, as if posing for a photo
spread in those old men's muscle magazines, or the ads in the back
of the glossy monthlies sold in 1960s-era supermarkets promising to
transform ninety-pound weaklings into supermen.

Where the woman working the machine next to me, on her back,
her legs held up by straps, scissoring her thighs open and closed, has
newly become a kind of in-law, in the way women in lesbian communities become related when our lovers are like brothers to one
another. In the Pilates room the teacher asks us questions about the
lesbians. How do we find each other? What do we mean by *lesbian
community*? My new sister-in-law and I try to respond, end up laughing. The gym teacher assumes we two lesbians are one kind of person

71

and she another, but really my new (and soon to be former) sister and I are not much alike.

What all three of us in the Pilates room have in common are our scars. In midlife women's scars are particular in that they tend to be located in the belly zone, the body's core, the center out of which our lives have been made, taken, enjoyed. The gym teacher had a C-section. My new friend had fibroids. I'm six months out from a full hysterectomy, middle body cut number three along a scar I've had since I was twenty, a narrow pink river running along the root of my stomach and the upper edge of my pubis. Our scars map what's happened between the beginning and the middle, the body flaws we've earned. We swing our thighs, the reformer whooshes, our scars throb, reminding us.

Underneath Is the Map of the Weathering of Storms / 2006 Minneapolis

Where after more than twenty years of shared love and calamity our wide living-room couch becomes our best love hotel. Lit up by the television, some film just done, Linnea lowers the living-room shade. One blond dog, Miss Rosemary, is asleep on the ottoman. The other blond dog, Miss Dusty, the one who gets nervous during storms, is scared too by our sex, so crawls to the top of the back cushions of the couch and pants. We ignore her heavy breathing and kiss harder, as Linnea pulls down the scooped front of my shirt to expose my breasts. We have been here before, but some of that was the old map, where Linnea had never been sick, where my sobriety had never slipped, where my fears of losing track of, or just plain losing, my lover were just heavy breaths against the unknown.

But this is the new map, where in twenty years our locations have changed. Our bodies have changed. Our brains have changed. Where once we came together like what? A jack and a trailer? A semi backing into a loading dock? Now we still need one another, but we're edgier with age. A pencil and a sharpener? An apple and a blade? Bodies change, pleasuring does not so much wane as deepen, and in spite of the warnings about married sex, about lesbian bed death, about women's libido at midlife, I want more now and climax faster and louder, and she is happier than ever to touch me, likes me to run my fingers down her tattoos, likes me to open my legs and gasp to her hand. Dusty pants, Rosemary runs in her sleep, the television light streaks our skin, and outside the sirens are not for us. She pulls down my top and I lift, so she can reach. We fit, still and changing, for more than twenty years, like any beloved's breast in her husband's mouth.

Underneath are maps that are torn away or stored elsewhere, maps of usual stories, of sobering up, of marrying, of calling a marriage a marriage, calling a queer marriage just a marriage, or a newer version of marriage made of both staying married and questioning the nature of marriage, that is both progressing and staying in place on a map of twenty years of some sickness, some health, on the south side of some city that keeps changing.

Underneath Is the Map of the Wasting / 1989 Minneapolis

Where I am driving down Lake Street, the main drag of South Minneapolis, in summer. June. It's hot and my windows are rolled down all the way and I am thirty years old, three years from my last drink.

Most of us carry the past around with us like a pop-up city. Turn a page and an old city springs to life. It's never the alabaster city that returns, not all progress and dream, not a bubble of what the city could be, if someone would finally just build it that way. No. It's always the Naked City. Six million stories. All of them gray and open in my chest, as I drive down Lake Street in summer, the liquor store lights streaking my face orange and yellow in the rearview mirror, the windows of Robert's Shoes, *Hardly a Foot We Can't Fit*, wild with the motion of a hundred dancing sneakers, pastel pimp loafers, work boots with twine-colored ties.

Traffic is caught up at the intersection because the liquor store is open on Friday nights until ten, so I sit in traffic and smoke the first cig

I've smoked in three years. I inhale slowly. My chest muscles clench, and if a stranger in a neighboring car has the nerve to look into my eyes I might look back. Hoping to see myself. Awake. Alive in the glassy light of another human's eyes. I am sleepy and I want to wake up. I am awake but I'd rather be on fire.

This is what I mean when I say I want the city alight inside me. I want to light myself up, and fast. In the heat. In the summer. My windows are rolled down and Lake Street is bumper to bumper. I can hear the salsa and rap and American pop oldies streaming out the windows of the neighboring cars. I can smell the cigarettes mingling with the hot tar of the street, and I can smell my own breath, dirty with smoke. I want to stick my head out the window and tangle my hair in the breeze of heavy traffic. I want to be drunk. Drink enough and the city will reach down and put her hand between your legs. Or so I think.

Underneath is the map of finding the one and falling in love, the map where we say, You are my one and only. The map of making the mistake of believing we are too happy to need further maps, that we are mapped, now, mapped forever.

Underneath Is the Map of the Wise Choices / 1988 Minneapolis

Where we are, of all places, in her mother's bed, our first trip back to Illinois together, for the holidays. I'd worn a silky red blouse from some Chicago resale shop, with a black leather miniskirt, and Linnea wore those tight jeans that made her thighs look so long and fine, and we'd taken silly snapshots of each other wearing fuzzy red Santa hats, lips oh-ed, our sounds, hohoho, both play and foreplay. Now, with her hand, she keeps on and on, because I want her to, rough enough that I bleed a little, onto her fingers, and we laugh because this is her mother's bed, her mother whom I already love and who already loves me. Linnea just keeps on because this is our time to map into each other, imprinting in blood.

Underneath Is the Map of the Withholding / 1985 Minneapolis

Where the woman I am sneaking around with stops by on her way home from work, just to talk, she always says, and we talk, some, until her hand is up my skirt. Even now I know she's not good for me any place but bed; even now I know she's a preliminary map, a woman with mannish qualities, my first butch. I won't remember how we get to tying each other to the bedposts with my scarves; I only know how badly I want her to tie me down harder, no please, harder, and though this will someday seem like nothing, late-night-cable-TV-cute, how sure I am now—in these pre-Internet, feminist sex wars times where the antiporn dykes and the pro-sex dykes yell at each other in the feminist magazines and snub each other in the streets—that I will never, ever, tell anyone. She does tie me harder, both ankles and wrists, until I gasp and beg her to touch me, and she will, but the longer she withholds the better. She controls the future I want but can't yet have, and so gives me some, but not all.

Underneath Is the Map of Wayfinding / 1982 Minneapolis

Where my résumé is limited: Inattentive waitress. Reluctant university news reporter. Shy community organizer. A twenty-something binge boozer looking to a new city for relief. So I move to Minneapolis from Illinois and immediately find a job in an Uptown pub with live music, burgers, and light-to-stout beer on tap.

And now this is the day I think I'm waiting on somebody big. Prince is not huge news yet, just a local boy done good enough to make it to the downtown record shop windows, striking a pose in bikini briefs on a narrow scroll of a poster, torso bared like a sex-positive Jesus hovering over the asphalt snow. I don't even know Prince's music yet, just pictures of his long-lashed face, his skinny cipher hips.

But that's advertising. In the pub the little man sits at a dim table wearing a cowl-neck sweater, pretty curls luminous in the olive candlelight, whispering when he orders soup. I'm not so much in awe as in hope of a big tip, enough to fund my after-work medications across the street at the Rainbow Bar, where I'll unbraid my hair at a dark bar table, watch cars and busses glitter past until closing.

It's years until Prince will refuse his own name and let journalists rewrite him as the Glyph. Prince will be, but isn't quite yet, the fashion maven of a generation, one of the inventors of what will be called the Minneapolis Sound—new-form funk, mixed-race dance pop, part post-Motown, part stoic Scandinavian American populist, part prime-time porno—the expression of an upper midwestern city I don't know well enough to hear yet.

Maps are not literal. Signs can only represent. The waitress is waiting for her life to change. The downtown bridge of Prince's city hangs sexy over the Mississippi as if suspended by stocking garters. Gay girls with asymmetrical bobs will, in a few years, hear about the little man's lesbian backup band, line up outside of First Avenue for a chance to groove in the dark like his Wendy and Lisa. Prince himself will keep resurrecting, rising from the steam of a claw-foot tub, naked as a saint, reaching toward the kids at home who want their MTV, as if wanting itself were holy. I don't know yet that the little man sipping soup in my station is not Prince, but a Prince performance, a soft-spoken karaoke, a professional Prince impersonator who won't even leave me a decent tip. I don't even know yet that Prince himself is more feminine than any female I will ever sleep with, those feet clad in stiletto-heeled boots, his voice a decibel louder than static.

Underneath Is the Map of Westering / 1980 Chicago

Where the woman who catches my eye must be a regular. She has reddish hair and a wrinkled neck and wears a black tuxedo. I've never heard of women who wear tuxedos, have no idea I will someday marry a woman who owns several. This must be a special night because this grand dame of the Ladybug Saloon is also wearing rhinestone earrings. She leans against the wall of the bar that's only as wide as a hallway. I stare at her work-worn fingers stroking a glass of amber booze, stare at her wiry red-gray hair, her creased face, her easy smile.

My own image is carefully constructed tonight: long hair braided in my singular fashion, four strands instead of three, my thrift shop sweater strategically ripped along the bra line, my stance wide, one hip jutting to one side, my body asymmetrical, signaling. *I am offbeat. I can take your shit.* Sexy slumming, pretending to be earnest and revolutionary, is gay girl chick-magnet fashion in 1980, although I won't admit I care about how I look.

My lesbian friends say I'm distant and experienced; they think I have mysterious lovers they haven't met, and I make sure not to correct them, but in reality, so far, I'm just looking. The woman I'm staring at in the Ladybug makes my insides whine like one of those weird Yugoslavian banjos the Croatian guys play at my dad's favorite joints, down on the East Side.

But this part of my mapmaking is all wrong, intentionally inaccurate. I wish the journey west were really that simple. You see a woman across the room. Your body vibrates in response, and you know who you are. The truth is I am only twenty-one, and I am at the Ladybug for the first time, and while I'd been to gay bars before this was my first all-lesbian joint, and while I know lots of lesbians I still haven't kissed one, not on the lips, not with an open mouth, certainly not with my teeth.

The Ladybug butch really is the first tuxed woman I've ever laid eyes on; I haven't even seen the famous Marlene Dietrich flick yet, slim hips careening between café tables as she leans over to light a lady's cigarette—so yes, when presented with the Ladybug's resident Dietrich, I can only stare. But it's a redhead across the room I'm really drawn to here, the one with mobster shoulders who shoots me a hard look that makes me want to kiss her and slap her, urges I don't then believe I'm right to feel, not according to the map of early 1980s feminism. It's easier, more acceptable, to pretend some sweet old school butch sees me then, the one whose hair is actually silver-gray. Not red.

Underneath Is the Map of Wanderlusting / 1979 Chicago

Where I meet Daniel, a longhaired radical guy, at another community organizing conference, just as I begin to wonder, Who will I kiss next? Woman? Man? Friend? Stranger? Tonight I'm drunk, the kind of drunk I love best, white wine high, loose, transparent, a white city alight in a wavering space, my body seemingly steady and statuesque as a lady in a fountain, that bare-breasted torso, the fountain's gushing center. Just drunk enough, but not too drunk, gesticulating, enunciating, long braids swinging with each whip of the neck, bare-faced—I am, on this part of the map, against cosmetics—flush with performance, making some little audience laugh with sharp jokes I will wish to repeat, later, except I'll never remember them.

This conference is in Chicago, the wine served in a suite of the Congress, a historical landmark from what I think of as my father's city, the hotel built for the Columbian Exposition, the year our great-grandfather Big Petar was born in Croatia, once a classy joint for the bustled, feather-hatted, and shiny-shoed set, but now shabby enough for downwardly mobile radicals to feel at home. I live three hours south in Urbana, where I'm working as a VISTA Volunteer community health care organizer, the stipend a whopping $300 a month, which in 1979 is enough, barely, to keep me alive. VISTA pays my way up to the city for these trainings run by perpetually exhausted 1960s politicos only half-convinced by their own workshops, based on Saul Alinsky's book *Rules for Radicals*, a primer for neighborhood campaigns to stop city-splitting freeways, development greed, and bad behavior by police. During the day we role-play in stuffy hotel meeting rooms, pretending to picket corporate board meetings or face off against corrupt aldermen or throw ourselves at demolition cranes. At night the wine is free.

When I meet Daniel in the Congress lobby on the last night of the conference he has his bicycle and his hair is tied back into a rippled ponytail. I'm wearing a khaki skirt, a T-shirt that stands for something, and modest kneesocks—long before kneesocks become a rock video fetish—which I wear because I've taken on the then-lesbian style of not shaving my legs but can't bear yet to let anyone see. I am drunk when we walk down to the lakefront, water peaking and falling under the bottoms of boats, drunk when we kiss, or when I think we are kissing. Later I will remember kissing and later still there will be letters. But tonight I go to bed alone, in a dark interior room overlooking an air shaft, careful not to wake a roommate who wears a hairnet and snores, as Daniel pedals south to his household of earnest twenty-something midwestern private college grads, the only white people still living in an old mill neighborhood just off the South Side lake shore, near the streets my mother had long ago made sure to leave.

What are the rules for radicals when it comes to touching one another? I am choosing to believe we can do away with rules. All I need is the right turn of phrase. Like with Daniel, a few months later, at the close of yet another VISTA training, a car full of newly schooled radicals, smoking too much, drinking too much, and me still proud to be able to smoke and drink just that much more, all headed toward Daniel's South Side house for a slumber party.

One of the guys in the car makes a joke while we're stopped at a red light, in a neighborhood where we are the only white people for miles, about how we ought to pile out of this car, run circles through the urban mist until the light pops green, Chinese Fire Drill he calls it, when Daniel, driving, says, *Now let's not be racist.* His polemics are my seduction, the reason I will end up in Daniel's bed, in the room strewn with so many young radicals, drunk and over-conferenced, spread out on rugs and in borrowed sleeping bags.

No matter that I've already picked out the women in Urbana I hope will be the first women I'll kiss. No matter all those half-sleeping witnesses. Daniel had done the one thing we all know never to do at a party: he'd inserted a moral tone, and maybe it was one of the rules for radicals but it was also something my father might do. The rules of my father, his thoughtful schoolteacher face and the deep imprint of his code, have always been, with women, with men, even in this moonlit room full of earnest and unseasoned radicals, my measure.

Outside Daniel's window the lake peaks and releases under the cold March night, and I am white city drunk again, or still. I can't say if Daniel invites me into his bed. Maybe I just climb in. My kneesocks flash in the moonlight. My bare thighs—when did I take off my skirt?—accept the narrow muscle of his torso, his hands on my breasts, his low shush, reminding me to be quiet because of the others, his hand reaching below, and I don't know why it takes me so long to notice that I am not the only woman he is kissing. When had his housemate, the dark-haired woman from some older city out east, climbed into bed with us? I see, by the whisper of his mouth meeting her mouth, that he has kissed her, more than kissed her, before. He kisses me. He kisses her. He kisses me again, against the scrapes and shuffling intakes of all those other radicals.

Daniel is so fair in his distribution of kisses. Odd that I don't wish to kiss her, the other woman, considering how badly I want to kiss a girl. But not this girl. Even now, drunk, and kissing, I see this is no accidental three-way. This is a power smack-down, a citizen action straight out of Alinsky's manual, outside interest versus neighborhood body shield, the identified leadership, the tremulous step up into amplified moment, two women intent on drawing contrary city maps. And Daniel, I wish more of him, but really I suppose he's just thinking what most guys would: Like wow, like two chicks, both in my bed. And that we all, despite such well-considered foreplay, keep our underwear on is due less to ethics than embarrassment, we two women noiselessly peaking into the palms of Daniel's hands in the presence of all the others who might be only pretending to sleep.

Daniel has somewhere to go in the morning, a road trip. He wakes me into grainy sun streaming in from his tiny lakeside window. Later I will stretch up to the tips of my toes to make out a green corner of the lake. The housemate is gone, back to her own room, I presume, and Daniel leans in close and whispers. Thank you, he says, low enough so as not to wake the others, chests rising and falling on all sides. Thank you, Daniel says again, and I nod, sober now. But does he mean thanks for the half-sex? For seeming not to mind that his housemate had horned in? For giving him his two-chick-for-one story, for my breasts in his hands?

Or thanks for understanding the rules, that *radical* is less person than word, and words are maps, and maps say more about where we think we've been than where we actually reside.

Underneath are so many incomplete maps of a Chicagoland childhood and adolescence, all the illegible moments and unmappable people who made and remade us, and the maps that made or remade their maps.

Underneath Is One Reconstructed Map of Wending / 1950 Las Vegas

Where before me, my Gram Rose, she had a friend, back in the old days. My Italian uncle, Rose's son-in-law, tells me the story. He's this Chicago city supervisor, my uncle says, the guy in charge of streets. Your gram was a classy lady back then, he says, and a widow alone with three kids. This politician meets her downtown after she gets off work, takes her to dinner at the swanky joints. It's good for him because he gets to go around with this beautiful dame on his arm. So this one time he invites Rose to Vegas, and once she's there she finds out she's the guest of all these Mafia guys, and they're delivering white roses to her room and treating her to the whole big-spender routine, and Rose, she's feeling a little uncomfortable, you know, taking money from mobsters.

So what does she do? I ask. I'm listening hard. I am redrawing my grandmother's map as he speaks, and therefore too my own.

Well, Rose wants them to know she's insulted. Who do these mobsters think she is? She pays her own bill, takes a taxi to the airport, and flies back to Chicago.

My uncle shrugs and laughs. We both love this map, Rose in old Vegas, a mobster moll, her white hair, styled in loose starlet waves falling back away from her face as she laughs, standing at some thick-shouldered gangster's back, the slot machine lights playing off her cheekbones. Is this the connected Chicago guy who buys her the mink jacket with her name embroidered into the lining and the blue topaz ring that glistens from her finger like a desert hotel swimming pool?

The part about refusing to take the money, marching home in a huff, the repudiation of any kindness that might tarnish her reputation, this part I fill in from old movies—Lauren Bacall, pensive in a slim-fitting dress the same blue as Gram's topaz, wary of accepting gifts from Robert Stack, leaving a neatly scented note before she flees. This is the sort of map Rose makes of herself. The woman who will not be sullied. The woman you can marry but cannot spoil.

But the map Rose lives? Who would she have been, under the rush and shatter of those lights, in the arms of a man who would take care of everything? I'm banking on the chase of Vegas neon, the click of her heels across the casino floor. I believe Rose, like me, must have had a hard time mapping herself straight home.

Underneath Are Reconstituted Fragments of a Map to the West/ 1930 Chicago

Where my other grandmother—Little Grandma, Mom's mother—marries a gutter drunk and moves to the South Side steel mill projects. Where Little Grandma's sister remaps herself into a downtown bottle blonde.

We know so little about my mother's extended family, from infrequent gatherings in bungalow basement rec rooms—macaroni salad, Jell-O mold, cigarettes, my mother's father drunk again, TV trays arranged in wide arcs under the electric beer signs lit up to resemble clean mountain rivers most Chicagoans only know from TV. *From the land of sky blue waters* the placards read, as a smiling bear cracks open a can of Hamm's. Polacks instead of the Croats and Bohemians on my father's side. Mill people. But everyone on the South Side of Chicago is a little bit mill people.

If I meet the Hollywood blond aunt in one of those basements I won't remember, but eventually my brother Paulie tells me stories, about the time he is the last kid still living at home, inheriting the job of driving Little Grandma and her sister to suburban malls, or meetings of the sisters downtown on State Street, where he helps them return

Christmas presents. One sister keeps two brown wigs on Styrofoam heads on the dresser of her apartment with the gray streaked windows and squeaky radiators. The other bleaches her hair electric.

The day I find out about the bottle blond auntie I am thirty-eight and it's raining, October at Holy Cross Cemetery in Calumet City, Illinois. This is the grayest topography of the gray side of the city, and on this gray morning we are putting Little Grandma into the ground. Our Lady of Czestochowa, every Polish cemetery's guardian, presides, as does the electrical grid just over the graveyard fence shadowing the plot where a cluster of my mother's people are buried, what looks more compound than garden of eternal rest, the gravestones flat granite tiles sunk into the grass. Aunt Lucy, my mother's blond sister in from California, the one who married well and left Chicago too, gestures to a marker with the pointed toe of her LA boot. Joanna Lussac. 1979.

Who's that? I ask.

Aunt Lucy says, This is my mother's sister. I don't get it. My great-aunt's name would have been Anna Luschak. Polish. Hard to pronounce. Hard to spell. Who is this Joanna Lussac? The name looks French.

Aunt Lucy laughs, throaty in the chill, holds her coat closed around her neck. Anna changed her name, Aunt Lucy says. I guess she thought this spelling was fancier. This Joanna is very beautiful, and wild for her time. Has a long affair with some Chicago politician. An alderman maybe? No one knows for sure. Gives birth to his son. None of her cousins will talk about it. Then one day blond Joanna dies in her sleep. I've tried to find out more, but no one's spilling.

Bottle-blond aunt. Another hootchy-kootchy politician's moll, in the days when all the Chicago politicians are crooked or connected or both. The blonde not ashamed to take the roses. White finger curls and strappy shoes flashing as she dances in a flouncy dress. Her hair a beacon in the motel moonlight.

Her body a ticket. West. Toward me.

FIG. 10. *Map of California Shown as an Island* by Johannes Vinckeboons, 1639.

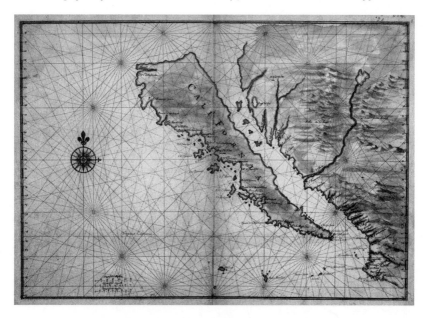

On clear days California appears as an island
of all our lost migration tales.

On a Clear Day, Catalina
Los Angeles itinerary, with overlooks and day trips

In San Pedro the trees dropped plum-colored petals into the streets. The industrial port of Los Angeles is better known for longshoreman dive bars, old-time European supper clubs, and the seedy streets of 1970s TV detective show chase scenes than for the beauty of its blooming trees. Still, it was the outrageous flowering I noticed first when visiting my little brother that May, just in time to see the trees lit up with blossoms.

TripTik Los Angeles: Like most military families, my brother Paulie, his wife, and their two kids move every two or three years, their migrations perpetual, their memories shaped like maps. Paulie's moves have led him around the world and back, through the neon commotion of Tokyo, across the cobbled fields and villages surrounding London, and into the mall-ways at the hem of Washington DC.

Everyone's maps stand in for something real, the city-like shape of some particular time of life, but no map shows the way Paulie and I remember the rumble and muck of Chicago, the city we both look for in all the other cities. This time the air force moved Paulie all the way west to LA, but the LA where he lives is the port of San Pedro, which in terms of immigration history may be the most Chicago-like location in the West.

Still, for our family, California is a new terrain. I visited Paulie this time at his home in an air force–owned neighborhood with an armed guard at the gate, an enclave hidden within the white fog of the Pacific Ocean. A fragment of the roiling sea was visible from the park up the hill from his block. On clear days he could see Catalina.

I'd come to LA to see my nine-year-old niece Adria, who had just decided to be a poet. She had one of those teachers that year: tall and well-tailored with hip eyeglasses and bolts of blond streaked through her hair, the type who had her mixed class of fourth and fifth graders reciting Emily Dickinson and T. S. Eliot. Here was a teacher who asked the children questions like *Which are the working words of this poem?* then cried and pressed her palm over her heart when she heard a lyric that moved her. I had come to hear Adria perform in her first poetry reading.

According to my sister-in-law Mitsuko, the morning of Adria's reading was like most mornings in San Pedro, cloudy and cool. My plane the night before had been crowded; once I arrived at my brother's house I was too keyed up to sleep, and in the morning I realized I'd forgotten to pack my hairdryer. Whose idea was it to schedule a poetry reading for 8:30 a.m.? I showed up at the school headachy, out of sorts, at the start of a bad hair day.

I didn't see Adria until I stepped into her classroom, just as the poetry was about to begin. It was not my idea to be her performance-day surprise. The kid had called me long distance, begged me to come. Once I'd worked out my travel plans I was dying to call her back and tell her. Of course, honey. I wouldn't miss it. I wanted her to know she could depend on me; I didn't want to play around with a little girl's longing. But my brother wanted me to surprise her.

If I were Adria this kind of surprise would have displaced me, disembodied me. But I attended fourth grade in a three-story brownstone box within smelling distance of the South Chicago mills. We had no poetry-wielding teachers. I was unaware as a girl that real people wrote books. I didn't meet a teacher who told me to write a poem until high school. What I learned as a girl, instead of the working words of poems, was to tell myself scratchy whispering secrets, which might be why I was a drinker before I was a writer.

I don't want to teach Adria to become the clouded and impossible-to-please girl I had been before I fled my home, but this wish may be more about me than her. She is already bilingual, no less at home in Kobe, Japan, with her mother's sisters than she is in her own living room. And Adria has teachers who ask her to read her poems in classrooms with doors hanging open to the Pacific fog, Catalina wavering on the horizon. In San Pedro the kids see whales at recess. No wonder they write poems.

Day Trip to the Old–Old Country

I've never been to our original family Old Country, but Adria has. She was still a kindergartner then, but might remember some sliver of Dalmatian shoreline, some bank of white stone wall overlooking the sea.

Adria was conceived near the Adriatic, the sea featured on the map as an expanse of blue between the long finger of the Dalmatian Coast and the outer shore of the Italian heel, extending all the way south to Greece. Adria may have retained some watery impression of her first return to her father's family homeland, the payoff of my brother's long drive from London, across Europe and down into the Dalmatian Coast, when she was just four, her little brother, Sava, still an infant. The drive south through Dalmatia to Dubrovnik is said to be one of the most gorgeous drives on earth. I envy her that trip, even if she barely remembers it.

What Adria actually recalls of the Adriatic is likely the sea depicted on a tourist's postcard, a view from the Italian side of the water. Her papa sent me the same postcard a year after their family vacation, when he was deployed. The scallop-edged photograph pictured an idyllic harbor, wooden boats setting in the slanting sun, afternoon shadows fingering the peeling bows. This was Cervia, where my brother prepared wills for NATO flyers before they set off to bomb Milošević's Serbia. It would have been wrong for my brother to send his family postcards of decimated Belgrade TV stations and the demolished Chinese embassy or any other image of detonation and debris, yet those safely anchored fishing boats don't tell the whole story of their papa's months away from home—nobody knew for how long.

I don't have a photo of my brother as a wartime lawyer, although I did see him at work on TV once; a Chicago news crew visited his unit in Italy and ran a story that featured him standing on a windy runway waving to the planes. I wasn't surprised they chose him as their human interest—South Side boy, at work, over there. He smiled and nodded in the wind of the tarmac when the reporter asked him questions. He's the type the camera likes. Most people like him too. Paulie and Linnea are similar that way, something inviting about their faces or stance that inspires strangers on buses, trains, airplanes, and the streets of unfamiliar cities to spill their life stories.

Everyone in our family has stories about Eastern European immigrant strangers who ask us about our last name—airline baggage handlers or waiters or foreign-language video store clerks who read the American spelling on a credit card or driver's license and routinely ask: Serb or Croat? But if the guy—and it's usually a guy—turns out to be a Croat himself? Paulie's the only one of us likely to bring him home for dinner, which is why I find it so hard to picture Paulie at work on that Italian airstrip in his combat greens, his long face smiling, scowling, waving to the flyers, hoping he got their wishes down right as they rocket off to bomb a city just a few hours' drive from the village where our grandfather Petey was born.

Adria is Paulie's older child, a bronze comma of a girl, named for the Mediterranean geography halfway between her parents' opposite continents. She is narrow and stands crookedly, like her mother, but is an extrovert like her father, getting bigger in front of an audience. My nephew Sava is the opposite, the shy one, a science whiz who never answers my questions and speaks to me only when he's in the mood. Both children straddle a divide, their father a U.S. Air Force man, their mother a citizen of Japan, their most accurate hometown map a light-up globe.

Historians say the story of the world is a roll call of migrations, which means world history is the history of longing for some alabaster city, a history of which my longing, Paulie's longing, Adria's longing are all a part.

Longing has a way of moving the body forward, that lean toward, that palpitating chest ache, desire a wheel. As in every family story our great-grandparents' longing set off a series of global reactions that have so far resulted in Adria and Sava, half-Japanese, half-Euro-American, residents of San Pedro, Los Angeles, USA.

And then we have those bombs, tying us, severing us from our pre-American past. Paulie's hand is aloft in the blue Italian air, his knuckles tan against a background of white smoke, the gust of departing planes. The Dalmatian islands scatter below the bellies of the bombers as the already broken Balkan cities zoom into range.

TripTik Los Angeles: My brother picked me up at LAX late on the night before the poetry reading, so late the usually crammed freeways of LA were wide open, bleary with smog and the periodic shimmer of headlights. The landscape looked like the misty and dim-lit panoramas I remember from a movie my friends and I—high school literary magazine and theater types—loved when we were eighteen, an overwrought and arty Alan Rudolph flick called *Welcome to L.A.*, about longing and sex, appetites never filled, and nasal Keith Carradine ballads that rhymed LA with decay. I'd been sleepy on the plane, but once I landed I felt buzzed up and cinematic, ready to ride into the lights. Welcome to these lost and smoky hills, LA, the capital of location-based longing.

It took about twenty minutes to get to San Pedro, the drive taking us not toward the LA dream machinery but away, Hollywood at our backs, the huge Port of Los Angeles looming before us. San Pedro is a community of immigrants; people come here to work, at the port if they're lucky, the largest container complex in the country. Three thousand ships a year dock there, each one carrying as many as five thousand cargo containers, those long rectangular crates that might be transferred onto a train, might be loaded onto the back of a transport semitrailer, might be unloaded right there, in full view of the Pacific. Most of Adria's and Sava's classmates, if they weren't air force kids, were children of the men and women who worked the docks.

Most mornings, after dropping the kids at school, Mitsuko joins the other mothers at the coffee shop up the hill. One mom who's a regular at their morning coffee circle works the night shift at the docks, driving a forklift; she grew up in San Pedro, as did her husband, who works the docks too. The other mothers are from Mexico or Colombia or Bosnia, their husbands the ones unloading those containers or standing in line for an application in the hopes of a chance to unload those containers. Their children speak English at school and learn their parents' home languages, Spanish or Serbo-Croatian or Japanese, at their dining-room tables every afternoon. This is not the LA of 1970s art films populated by white people with too much money, too much time, and too much sex. This is more like the Brooklyn of Elia Kazan, a cleaned-up version, crowded with mothers mad at their husbands, with workers who remember their Old Country, with people who all know each other because their kids know each other, who all wanna be a contender.

And the morning I was there the kids wanna be contenders too. They wanna be in show biz. I filled up the door of Adria's classroom and lingered there, looking for my niece. She sat on the floor with her classmates, some dressed as T. S. Eliot's Jellicle cats, some in baseball hats for their roles in the reading of "Casey at Bat." Adria's long hair grazed the classroom tile as she leaned forward to whisper in a classmate's ear, the brown tips bleached blond by the California sun and grown longer in the year since I'd seen her last. She had new glasses, purple cat's eyes, the same shape as mine. When I'd visited the previous spring she'd asked me, Auntie, why do you wear those strange glasses? Now she had a pair of her own.

When she finally saw me I noticed her blink. The purple specs accentuated her pretty eyes, wide and expressive, from the Croatian side but also recognizably Japanese, her mother's daughter. When it sunk in that her auntie had shown up for the show, just in time, Adria smiled secretly. She looked away, pretending to pay attention to the teacher, then looked back at me, grinning, Paulie hovering over my shoulder with the video camera running.

Point of Departure: Body and Water

Longing for language. Longing for locations. These are twin long-ings. A single well-chosen word can cause us to rearrange ourselves. Cognition is a bloom that opens under the skin. We become what we come to know.

Linnea and I have a long-running joke when one of us can't think of the word for something, a quotation from the film *The Miracle Worker*. The teacher, her hair and waistcoat tied up tight, her eyes obscured by tinted eyeglasses, spells out words into the open palm of the young deaf, dumb, and blind Helen Keller, as water sputters out of a pump. W-A-T-E-R. It has a name, the teacher repeats. The fingers of Helen's free hand listen to the movement of the teacher's lips. It has a name. When she finally makes the connection—that this seemingly random collection of movements, of pulses in her palm, has a meaning, refers to this encounter between the body and water—young Helen is ecstatic. She leaps into the satisfaction language brings to longing, laughs, falls into the arms of her teacher because she knows now that *it* has a *name*.

Point of Destination: Geography of Corners

Some films have a way of making unhappiness appealing, and as a teenager I found the smog of Alan Rudolph's LA a titillating haze. The characters, all of them bereft, navigated the city with endless talking, so many words, the wide, hilly spaces of language.

Just one character, played by the gap-toothed supermodel Lauren Hutton, was silent, a photographer obsessed with shooting pictures of architectural corners, her eye pulled to images of endpoint and entrapment. Her character was what led me, as a young woman, to wander around Chicago photographing strangers' feet, obsessed, I would have said, with incompleteness. But what I really wanted was to step into Lauren Hutton's celluloid body, so lean in her billowing white palazzo pants—so compellingly speechless, her beauty made strange and off-center by the gap in her smile.

TripTik Los Angeles: I sat in the corner of Adria's classroom as the citizens of White Point Elementary's fourth and fifth grade became dancing cats. They were Casey at Bat. They were frowning or giggling poets reading their own poems that began with the word *never*. Their tall teacher teared up when she read a few Emily Dickinson lines, one thin hand held over her heart as if she were pledging to the flag, and then it was Adria's turn. Her poem surprised me; it was about a spooky carriage with flailing horses that pulled her into the pitch of midnight, their destination the middle of the sun. Adria's lips twitched when she read, the same way they'd twitched when she was four and I watched her perform in her first ballet recital.

Is it unusual for California grade-schoolers to write poems about death? One girl in Adria's class read a sad poem about losing her mother to cancer, but most of the kids were writing about dogs, sports, family dinners. Was Adria's poem what comes of mixing Harry Potter with Emily Dickinson so early in the day? Adria was a good student, swayed by the fascinations of her teachers. What she made was formed by where she made it, her poems no exception.

Once during her year in a DC Catholic school I asked Adria what she wanted more than anything. She drew her face out long and pressed her lips together. Peace in the Whole World, she said. She said the word *Peace* as if the word itself were a prayer, slick and round as a rosary bead. But what did the word *Peace* mean then to a Catholic grade-schooler who lived on the peripheries of U.S. Air Force bases, in U.S. Air Force officers' neighborhoods with armed soldiers at the gate, to a girl who had never seen an actual war but had missed her father when he left home to wave at the bellies of those bombers? She couldn't see the current war from where she lived, and the base where her father worked had not been deployed to Iraq, not yet, though they might go at any time. One of the White Point Jellicle cats was the son of a journalist who had not been back from Iraq in months.

Was Peace a place bordered by the low groan of the church organ and the pitch and swoon of the choir, by a prairie of nuns mumbling prayers, by cities of men who all dressed like her father, in green and black military fatigues? Adria's poem ended in an image of entering the sun, suggesting arrival into the final peace, but where did she think that was? In cinematic LA? In the belly of the solar system? On the shores of Catalina?

Day Trip to Before Atlantis

Catalina is a tourist destination, a day trip the moms of Adria's school talk about taking but keep postponing. At coffee after the poetry reading, they will talk about it again: the boat cutting through the churning current, the wind on their faces, blowing their hair free from clips and bands, the green blur of the shoreline coming into focus. No, they won't really talk about the wind. They will talk about whether they can trust their husbands to get the kids to school on time, whether their mothers and fathers-in-law will still be in California, or back home in Mexico, in Colombia, in Sarajevo. They will take a ferry to get to Catalina. They will have lunch. The blue churning waters, the wind, is what I will see in their smiles, the fog that rolls into their eyes as they talk, a whole day with nothing to do but go to Catalina, no duties at school, away from their San Pedro kitchens, swept away to the hootchy-kootchy island the swimsuits are named after. Catalina is their isle of joy, materializing out of their watery horizon like the lost city of Atlantis, speckled with sea salt.

Day Trip to After Atlantis

Catalina is not the only island within view of San Pedro. The other island is artificial, originally a mudflat and now a perfect rectangle, located half-and-half across the harbors of LA and Long Beach. Now it's an industrial warehouse zone, shipyards, and the federal penitentiary known for jailing both Al Capone and Timothy Leary, so a warehouse of organized vice and organized vision—but once, before, it was another place entirely, the immigrant village of Furusato.

First- and second-generation Japanese once made their homes on Terminal Island, convenient to their work in fisheries and canneries. The people of the island village of Furusato formed a half-and-half culture, no longer fully Japanese, not quite American. They spoke a mixed English/Japanese dialect. Their island village was isolated and idyllic, a hybrid space where they celebrated both American and Japanese holidays. They named themselves Yagore, which means dirty and ragged on the outside but clean and pure within. Who knows what names they would have eventually made for themselves if the United States during World War II had not issued Executive Order 9066, the rule of Japanese internment. The residents of Furusato were shipped to Manzanar in the California desert. While they were gone the U.S. Navy bulldozed their homes.

Now Terminal Island is a vanished village, a memory city, yet on a clear day you might be able to see the ghost bustle of a neighborhood, the men leaving early to fish, the children screeching in the dusty streets, the Americanized teenagers coming home in threes and fours from their day at San Pedro High School. If they were like most American teenagers they were more interested in dance music and the right kind of shoes than the war looming on the other side of the sea fog, still too far away to see. If they were like my grandfather Petey, born in one country, coming of age in another, they would have longed for little more than to come into focus, their inner purity becoming outer, their new America begging them to stay.

Day Trip to the Forgotten City

Paulie, like me, has never been an early riser, but in San Pedro he likes to breakfast before sunrise at the fish joint down by the pier. Where else in America would he find old Croat fishermen who come from the same region of Croatia where our grandfather was born? These are immigrant white guys in their eighties or nineties with wind-chapped faces and a store of dirty jokes, still working a few mornings a week when the catch is promising and the sky is clear of storms.

The morning after Adria's reading Paulie will drag me out to the pier with him. Another too-early morning for me. Paulie wants me to meet his old Croat pal, some stand-in for our grandfather Petey, or at least our grandpa's imaginary cousin. Zlatko or Goran or Nikola will be his name, this man with stiff white hair, the same texture as our father's, but his face rougher, his pores bigger, his jaw looser. He will be a guy who spent his life with boats and bottles. He won't be a college man like our dad, won't have spent his life talking to rooms full of high school kids. He might be the kind of guy whose own kids no longer talk to him, a guy who will talk anyone who will laugh at his jokes. He will love it when my brother comes in to see him, Captain Paulie with the Croatian surname, that air force guy from Chicago.

Zlatko will pat Paulie on the back. He is one of the few remaining Old School Guys. A Classic Guy. So Paulie will say to Zlatko: This is my sister. From Minneapolis. Zlatko will shake my hand but won't meet my eyes. These guys my brother befriends—they are always guys—are never the type who meet a woman's eye, so right away I'll have issues. These guys are also always the type to mispronounce the names of cities they have never seen. *From Minnie-an-apolis you say? Ah, Minnie-an-apolis. I knew a guy once from Minnie-an-apolis. Or was it Indiana-apoplis? Oh no, it was Doolooth. Is that near you?*

It won't matter whether or not I try to explain. No no, Duluth is three hours' drive north. Minneapolis is bigger, half of a double city; it shares the river with Saint Paul I'll say. Zlatko will nod, but he won't be listening. He will go on to talk about how he lives alone. Downtown San Pedro. Next to the Italian store, across from the Croatian Supper Club. Did we know there are more Croats in San Pedro than anywhere else in the American West? Did we know the Chicago Cubs used to train on Catalina? He won't mention all those Japanese who don't live here anymore. He won't mention that all the new Croats and Slovenians and Bosnians who'd come here recently were escaping a war that was in some ways the same war Zlatko ran from when he came over, as a boy, in 1924, or '34, or '44. Then he'll roll headfirst into a joke.

There was a Jew, a priest, and a limp-wristed fellow, he'll say. I'll wince and kick Paulie under the table, and Paulie will narrow his eyes at me as if to say, So what if Zlatko is some kind of jerk? Can't you see he's a friend of mine? Paulie's an expert in befriending jerks. Paulie sees not so much a jerk as a foggy forgotten port. A lost city he longs to save. The shadows of a history that will quickly lose form in the Catalina fog if Paulie doesn't show up for these early morning breakfasts.

Zlatko, with his unfocused gaze and shaking hands, reminds Paulie, and me too, of some character from our South Side of Chicago childhood, a black-and-white newsreel always playing at the back of our brains, a location Paulie's kids will hear about but never step foot in, just as Paulie and I can travel back but never really step foot in Kata and Big Petar's Croatia.

I wonder if jerks are nothing if not world-class longers. Those old-time jokes as told by jerks might not even be about what they seem to be: hate for the queers, the Jews, the latest round of foreigners. Not entirely, even if I can't help but experience them that way. They're an old way of talking, see, an old way of laughing that's lost in the fog.

To Paulie, Zlatko is the body the migrant loses by making the choice to move, and thus he is some part of Paulie's body, some history Paulie longs for. And if Zlatko is my jerk, I might be his. Another woman who won't laugh at his jokes. Paulie will squint because he'll be thinking I've got no respect, this guy coulda been our grandpa, or if not then somebody's grandpa, and what's he got besides his stories? What's it to me if this guy's a jerk? Zlatko's hands will hover over the table as he leans forward to deliver the punch line. His coffee will be cold, he's been talking so long. When he leans into the table the cold coffee will splash over the rim of the cup, spill out into the saucer. I will sigh and lean forward to listen, even though I'm sure I'll regret it.

Point of Destination: Such a City

I never wanted to live within the city of Zlatko's punch lines. I longed, as a young woman, for life in the better city where ambition leads.

Here's a scene I daydream, not in the Rudolph film. The wide fabric of the photographer's palazzo pants ripples in the wind off Catalina. She stands on a dock, on a boat, on the shoreline. When she smiles the sun shines between her teeth. Her back is to the water. The city gathers in the lens of her camera. She leans forward to capture it all in the frame. The shutter clicks. Her hair twists back behind her. No words. Just destination.

Years after my adolescent obsession with celluloid Lauren Hutton, I sat, one table over, from the actual Lauren Hutton in a New York City restaurant. I recognized her with a start. She was older, of course, but still oddly beautiful. She ate alone. When she noticed me noticing her she smiled shyly and repositioned herself in her seat, the way one would who is used to being recognized but not all the time, and not as often as she had been once.

When the object of a long-held gaze catches your eye, gazes back, the gaze returned becomes a loop, a refrain, less migration than a circular route, no longer a progression toward but instead a meditation of being. I will never again be the lean young woman with the camera, and neither will Lauren Hutton. And so we meet. In this corner.

TripTik Los Angeles: The thing about San Pedro is the air is damp and a little bit salty. The thing about San Pedro is the Japanese who used to live here are gone, and now Mitsuko and Adria and Sava are here instead, half-and-halves, as Mitsuko likes to call them, along with others like them, the children of both Japan and the U.S. Air Force, and this is southern California so they know they don't have to drive far to find strip mall after strip mall selling food or furniture, toys or kitchen utensils from Japan. The thing about Chinese, Japanese, Vietnamese, and Korean strip malls that ring suburban LA is so little English is spoken in the course of a day it's hard to understand why anyone still thinks English is the first language of America. The thing about San Pedro is the port itself is a landing pad for goods that ship from companies called Hankyu or Hanjin or Maersk, steel containers lifted from the back of cargo ships, suspended from the arms of cranes, containers as long as house trailers piled up along flats of the Port of Los Angeles, little cities of unpacked goods. The thing about San Pedro is it's not the same LA as the one I've seen in the movies, not the LA where the studio execs or wannabe actors or glam lesbians live. My gay friends in West Hollywood are not even sure where San Pedro is on the city grid.

On the map San Pedro is part of the yellow spread of the city, but pastel passages of suburbia separate it from the rest of the metropolis. San Pedro is not the part of LA that rioted, nor is it the part up the hills that routinely catches fire. San Pedro might be the LA of old episodes of *The Rockford Files*, but it's not the LA of Alan Rudolph films about too skinny, too sexually disaffected, too rootless people. It is the LA of an old kind of longing, the kind Paulie and my old relatives who worked the South Side of Chicago mills and train yards used to know. The thing about San Pedro is that the goods flow in, the goods flow out, while most of the city doesn't notice, and the children show up for poetry readings, and the trees, the trees are crazy with blooming.

And what do I long for, here among the purple blooms of San Pedro, in the light of my niece's poems, in sight of Catalina? I've come for more than Adria's poetry. I've come to remember the feeling Adria doesn't even notice she feels, that necessity of stepping into the breeze pushing toward us from Catalina, that need to be a wheel. Leaving home, forgetting home, waging war with home, remaking home might all be stops on the itinerary of the same migration tale, just as my need to show up to see Adria read her poetry might be as strong as her wish to see me there.

Adria relaxed after she finished reading, her particular moment of stardom passed, and then she was just another among the White Point

Jellicle cats, prancing on tiptoe across the polished classroom floor, stroking her pipe-cleaner whiskers. My mind drifted to my soon-to-be future, espresso and rolls with Mitsuko and the other Jellicle mothers, up a steep hill from the school. Outside the open classroom door a spring breeze stirred the trees and petals spun into the streets. The children of White Point Elementary leaned over their reading and arithmetic, as some of their parents worked the harbor, loading or unloading freight from Japan or Germany or Kuala Lumpur. As some of their parents, escaped from wars they didn't make, bussing the tables of restaurants owned by the grandsons of the immigrants, the same immigrants who'd come here to escape wars they didn't make. As some of their parents tightened bolts and polished wings of the wars none of them can see from here but that play in the background, walls falling, holes opening in somebody's flowering streets.

Adria might see some but not yet all of the wars when she looks out toward the sea from the hills of San Pedro. She sees the same wavering shore of land, green and inviting, as the first sailors arriving from Dalmatia must have seen, as well the first fishermen from Japan. She sees a city of stacked containers and a bridge to Long Beach and cruise ships and freight barges, and she sees Catalina. Petals fill the San Pedro streets, and later I will talk about the tree around the corner from the school that's surrounded by mounds of purple petals the same color as Adria's glasses, and Adria will say, Auntie, I saw that same tree today.

We all need to see the blooming trees, and when they are gone we need to lean forward, or back, and long for them. I will wish I knew what kinds of petals these were. I'd like to teach Adria the working words for all these trees, all this blossoming.

FIG. 11. *Group of Slumless, Smokeless Cities* by Ebenezer Howard, 1898.

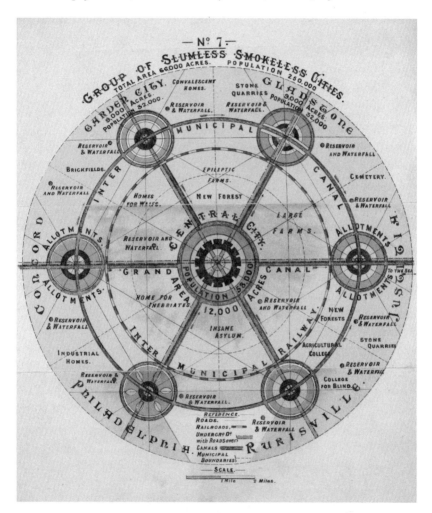

I have often longed to live in an impossibly geometric city.

Cities of Possibility

I knew my little city then mostly at night. It was my first spring in Minneapolis, when I waited tables at a south side music pub that served
food until bar closing—1 a.m. in those days. It was usually after 2 a.m.
before I finished side work, cashed out for the night, and headed home
smelling like beer. Sometimes I caught the last 21A bus trolling east
on Lake Street, in 1981 still a dim stretch of used car lots and pawn
shops. I got off at 17th Avenue, just before the cemetery, and walked
four barely lit blocks north to my apartment in a wobbly old duplex
that has long since been torn down.

My boyfriend Leonard lived two houses over. He's the one who'd
asked me to follow him to Minneapolis, then introduced me to this
beat-up part of the city populated by all sorts who couldn't afford the
rent in most other neighborhoods even then, when rents citywide were
still cheap. I say Leonard was my boyfriend, but man friend would be
a better way to describe who he was to me. I was just twenty-two but
he was thirty-five, not at all a boy. He was probably awake those nights
when I rolled in near 3 a.m., and he was probably drinking, as was his
habit. I might have gone to him, but most of the time I didn't.

This was the spring I began avoiding sex with Leonard, but that
wasn't why I didn't go up to see him. I can't think of any good reason

for refusing his company, except that I was day by day pulling away. When I did climb the narrow wooden stairs that led up to his kitchen door, I would find him sweetly drunk, and I would smoke a few of his cigs and we would drink together, listen to music, pre-born-again Dylan or maybe the Eagles, until we both fell asleep. In the morning Leonard would make me that dark cinnamon tea I loved, and I would drink it while wrapped in a quilt covered in a heavy cotton duvet—Leonard was the one who taught me the word *duvet*. I sat up on his futon, leaned back against his pillows, read his books, smoked more of his cigarettes. Leonard gave me nothing to complain about. But mostly I'd stopped coming over late, detaching from him and from my coworkers, who were clearly as baffled as I was regarding whether I was gay or straight or something else they couldn't name.

In the 1980s nobody I knew just asked a person if she were gay, and even if they had I'm not sure what I would have said. I'm a lesbian with an old hippie gentleman friend? Or perhaps the thing to say would have been: I will be gay as soon as I meet some lesbians, and by the way, do you know any? But that sounds too simple. Sometimes we seek out lovers because we long to be not more comfortable, but less. I started up with Leonard when I was nineteen because I wanted to change from who I'd been before him. He was older and knew about politics and living outside the lines and the best places to buy beer by the case. Now I was getting ready to change again, but first I had to leave him.

But not yet. Hovering on the cusp, longing, hesitating, I hedged, silently mooned over women at work I knew were too straight to want to kiss me, and after work walked around the indigo city at night, curiously unafraid. I imagined myself invisible, a wisp of fog walking into blue, although that must not have been true; someone must have seen me. Once, on my way in after work, before I changed my clothes and went out again, I heard my downstairs neighbors, middle-aged, party-hardy gals who were up all night too, blasting music, drunk and bellowing, describing me to one of their guests as I climbed up the back way into my apartment. She's *stacked*, I heard them say, and I was shocked to hear myself described this way—as visible, as female, as a vulnerable body.

In my waitron drag, the ubiquitous white shirt and creased black pants, I felt anything but stacked. All my neighbors knew about me was what they could see: I was young, too much alone, and too shy to accept their offers to drink with them. What they couldn't have known is I was less stacked than stuck, in sexual identity limbo, between multiple possibilities, all of them muted. I'm not sure I understood that I had that much of a body, of any body, especially not at night when I was walking.

Sometimes I walked around until dawn, once all the way from the east side back to Uptown where I'd boarded the bus after work, something like five miles, never once considering that someone would see me, a woman, walking alone, some idea in my head that I would buy breakfast when I got there, which never happened because it was too early and everything was closed. I liked Minneapolis best in the dark, when its shadows were exposed. Those were the times my new little city felt most like Chicago, and thus the time I best recognized myself, or at least some self I had been once, or thought I had been.

I never meant to move to Minneapolis. A program that aired on the Twin Cities community radio station at the time was called *Little City in Space*, which was precisely how I thought of Minneapolis. A pocket metropolis, floating in the undefined blue of the cold part of the Midwest. I'd come to Minneapolis from central Illinois because Leonard had begged me to and because the town where I'd started and dropped out of college was so flat, so muggy.

Maybe I should've gone back to my home city as I'd always meant to do. Maybe I could've gotten a job at the Earl of Old Town, the folk club on the near North Side of Chicago where Bonnie Koloc used to sing about how she always fell for lying, blue-eyed men, and every night before last call the white-bearded Earl himself came out to say, *Tip your waitress. She works hard.* I could work hard for tips. But I was still too afraid that if I returned to Chicago my family would drag me back to some version of the Old Country, turning me into what? Not the body my body wanted to be.

Before moving north I spent nights in my college-town apartment, up late, usually stoned, watching reruns on a little black-and-white TV my mother had given me so I wouldn't be lonely. When I finally fell asleep, I was invariably woken up again between 2 and 3 a.m. by a phone call from bearish, sheltering, absent Leonard. He'd moved ten hours' drive away without asking me what I thought about it, but once he got to Minnesota he decided he missed me, and by 2:30 a.m. or so he was drunk. He called and I picked up. He cried. He said he loved me.

It mattered that he told me he loved me. No adult man or woman, whether I'd slept with him or her or not, had ever loved me. Furthermore he was the one who believed so devotedly in nonmonogamy yet still called me to cry that he needed me, just me. That mattered. I still believed then that people were most honest when they were drunk, and so when Leonard was drunk I believed myself most lovable.

When I'd visited Leonard in Minneapolis, before the phone calls and the crying, he sat across from me at a light-speckled restaurant table in the glass-encased crystal court of the IDS center downtown, looking too bushy for the city in his curly beard and red flannel vest. I was twenty by then, my long hair braided, wearing painter's pants and a frayed, faded blouse, that late 1970s hippy-chick style that I was a half year or so from trading in for motorcycle boots and purple tights and 1950s housewife dresses. I must have chosen the right outfit for the occasion because that's when he told me. *Not* that he loved me, no, not that, not yet. What he announced was that he considered me *primary*, which in his relationship ethos meant, as far as I could tell, something like number one wife. That mattered to me as much as it confused me.

Later on, his predawn calls, which always lasted for an hour or more, left me sleep-deprived, drugged out on the slurred affection in his voice. Of course, I promised to move to Minneapolis, to live near him, to be lovable. A blue city. A glass city. The wild blue yonder.

All cities are really double cities: the city itself and another city, the city of possibility, a projection of the real, the manifestation, part practical, part erotic, of what we wish for in our lives. Or what I wish for. Some people, I know, pine for wild blue open spaces.

It's the possible city, the blue glass city, that I remember when I look back to my first year in Minneapolis, walking all night through the streets alone or with one of my first and most fleeting friends, a young man I waited tables with for a few months. If I couldn't find lesbians in the late-night restaurant world, gay men were easy enough to come by. When I did see lesbians, the obvious ones, with short hair and loose-fitting jeans who came into the pub for a burger, they didn't recognize me because I didn't look like them, couldn't bring myself to shave off my long blond hair. Waitresses in the early 1980s, even in the young Uptown joints, needed to look like girls to have any hopes of making tips. Besides, I never felt androgynous enough to adopt the halfway-between-boy-and-girl persona that was still the lesbian uniform in 1981. Gay men and I, on the other hand, had long gravitated toward each other; I would have been a fag hag had I stayed straight.

My new friend's name was Scottt—spelled with three *t*'s. He never told me if the final *t* was his own addition, but I assumed so. I'd changed by then into the kind of girl who wore eclectic thrift shop ensembles and lived in cheap city apartments with bad locks. He was the kind of guy who took money from older men and spent his rent on tickets to Diana Ross concerts. If you had asked me then, I would have said I was, in that and any friendship with a pretty gay man, like Sally Bowles of *Cabaret*, a fabulous bad girl with funny clothes, a foul mouth, and a pull toward the night. I would have been happy living in some hovel of a city boardinghouse with dusty draperies and neighbors in trouble, greeting my friends in a lacy camisole, falling in love with boys who didn't sleep with girls. If I couldn't finally decide to be a lesbian, that would do.

Scottt and I wandered through the sleepy streets of Minneapolis, still then a place that seemed to empty out at night. Life was not a cabaret here, not for Scottt or me. The silence was so deafening we could have been walking through a tunnel. We strolled down the center of Franklin Avenue and rarely met an oncoming car. Today I would be hard-pressed to find a major thoroughfare of the city so supernaturally quiet, but in those days in Minneapolis there were fewer people, fewer cars, fewer lights. The blue glass of the IDS tower throbbed dimly, but the windows of all the houses and apartments were dark.

Earlier that night, drinking wine in Scottt's apartment on the west side of the city, he gave me a ripped red wool jacket with a black satin lining and elastic at the cuffs and waistband. He'd worn it the last time he saw Diana Ross in concert. I wore it that night, and then for years more, until it was threadbare. I still keep it in my closet, decades after I've lost track of Scottt. The jacket helps fix him in my memory, a tall boy/man, his fine hair curling along the nape of this neck, his fingers more befitting a piano player than a waiter, talking about lovers and apartments and Diana. I'm not certain anymore if he showed me some of Diana's moves, that wave of first the shoulders and then the hips as she approached the mike, her arms flung out to her sides, her flat palms facing out, stopping all comers in the name of love. It may be Diana herself I remember, as Scottt conjured seeing her on the stage, or it may be that Scottt showed me with his own arms and hips how she did it. Either way, it was 3 a.m., and while the streetlights were too sporadically spaced to look like spotlights they still dappled the damp, early morning avenue. Scottt, me, and the shadow of Miss Diana walked through the night, marking the shadow hours of this little city with our dreams of some bigger, bluer place.

The emerald city. The alabaster city. Cities of crystal, cities of light, cities as the nexus of the hinterlands, cities as the queer metropolis, cities as the holy grail of immigration. Cities as the architecture of longing.

Frank Baum is said to have created Emerald City of Oz after repeated viewings of the world's fair alabaster city. Whatever his thoughts about Chicago's temporary city of dreams, he also lived in the actual gray city of Chicago, so he must have known the difference between the dream and the real, must also have seen the dream city's potential as metaphor, as the end of an odyssey, as Dorothy's destination of escape. In the film version of the *Wizard of Oz*, Emerald City sparkles on the far side of a landscape of poppies. In Baum's novel the dazzle is so bright that anyone who crosses its threshold must wear green-tinted sunglasses. But first the walkers have to cross a plain of sleep-inducing poppies. The danger of stopping short of the dream is a sleep so deep the city will always shimmer out of reach.

As a young woman I too knew the difference between the dream city and the real city. In the real city the bus was always late. The old Pinto I owned didn't start in the winter, and when I wasn't able to move it after a blizzard it was towed. On some weekends business at the restaurant was so slow the manager let me off early, before I'd made enough tips for rent, or I spent what money I did make drinking across the street from work, at the Rainbow Bar. There had been a brutal gay bashing in the city that winter that had made all the papers. One of the cooks I worked with, a short blond man, his hair cut in a jagged shag, was always nice to me, which in a commercial kitchen where the cooks and waitresses spent most of the night screaming at one another mattered a great deal. Then one night he told me he had been one of the guys who had beat up that fag. Why was he telling me this? Was he boasting? Was he lying? Was this some twisted way to find out if I was a dyke? I couldn't think of anything to say at first, then I started screaming at him to shut-up-shut-up. He stared at me placidly as I shrieked. That was the last time we talked about anything but my food orders. This was the real city.

The dream city was more of a beacon than an address. It was like the song the people of Emerald City sing as Dorothy and her friends approach the great green gates. *You're out of the woods, you're out of the dark, you're out of the night. Step into the sun, step into the light.* I wasn't out of the night yet, but I believed I would be. That's why I walked, even after spending a whole night working on my feet. Even on no sleep and eating only what I could scrounge at the restaurant. I kept on walking, my destination the most glorious place on the face of the earth.

Though my family story is a series of migration stories, lots of Croats stayed on the iron and copper ranges where my great-grandparents worked near Chisolm, Minnesota, and Calumet, Michigan. Some of their descendants are there still, plucking out Tamburitza orchestra laments on teardrop-shaped guitars from Croatia, Serbia, Slovenia, attending polka mass on Sundays, a few of them working what's left of the mines and taconite plants, some of them, as in any factory or mining town, holding the tavern stools in place. But my great-grandparents, Kata and Big Petar, with what was then their family of three little boys, kept moving until they got to the far southeastern side of Chicago, South Deering, the East Side, another community of Croats, Serbs, Slovenians, Poles, and Italians, another region called Calumet. Once they arrived in Chicago, Kata never moved again.

It's hard for me to understand why Big Petar came so far and traveled so many routes only to keep leaving again, but Kata may have done no better by staying put. Perhaps in middle age she tied her long dark hair back into that severe ponytail because she was done with longing. Or maybe she was just another pissed-off immigrant wife tired of her roving husband. Perhaps Big Petar remained loose-boned longer, full of drink and story, because his gaze was fixed on a distance he just couldn't get to, until his eyes took on the look of so many of the men done in by the mills and the mines.

The divorce certificate from the Superior Court of Cook County, Illinois, states that Petar and Kata *were lawfully joined in marriage on or about the 7th day of January 1906 A.D., at Brinje, Croatia, Austria.* According to family records, Big Petar was age twelve, Kata fifteen. The document goes on, a skeleton of facts. *Subsequent to their intermarriage the Defendant willfully deserted and absented himself from the Complainant without any reasonable cause for the space of over two years.* When he was no older than twenty-seven, the same age I was when I fell in love with Linnea, Big Petar left his wife and children on the Lake Michigan mill shore, fleeing westward, to his final Croat gathering point, those copper mines of Butte, Montana. The knots of his matrimony, first secured in a tiny town in Croatia, were unbound in Chicago, Illinois, USA, in October 1926.

Good riddance is what I imagine Kata must have said. So let him sleep in a hard bed with his stinking countrymen. His last new world was a boardinghouse where he lived with other Croats who never learned to speak English, eating the food cooked by someone else's wife that tasted just like the food back home, until he died of silicosis, that industrial worker's disease caused by breathing in too much mine dust; after years of mining copper, then iron, then copper again, his lungs disintegrated to russet sand.

So Kata sat out the rest of her days—as her daughter-in-law Gram Rose once described her to me—steely in her hard chair, by the window, looking out onto muddy Torrence Avenue, where the trolley screeched north into the arcade of South Chicago, south into the green surf of still-unplowed prairie. She sat watching, waiting for her boys to come home from the mill with their pay. Her oldest, Petey, the one who had squeezed her hand so tightly she had to shake him free the morning they stepped off the boat, was a good boy. He always brought home his money right away, never stopped at the tavern downstairs like the other boys did, like Big Petar had. The younger boys, those Americans, came home singing and swearing with words she couldn't understand, except by the crazy way they laughed, the way their father used to laugh when he was drinking. Kata sat stiff as a girder, hard as the glass of her window. The city outside was gray with the palpable possibility that this would turn out to be it, her new American life.

Queers, ostensibly the most un-American of Americans, are really more classically American than anyone else because of the way we know how to step into the light. Change is, after all, our special province. This is what I am thinking twenty-five years after I walked the blue city streets, when Linnea and I go to a drag show at an international meeting of drag kings held in a plush conference hotel in Minneapolis. In queer culture the light is sometimes an actual spotlight trained on a hotel banquet room stage.

The girl whose turn it was to show us her stuff wore a plain blue bandana, lace-up black punk-girl boots, and a slim denim skirt. Linnea had wandered back to the bar, blending in among the kings, although she was here, like me, as a spectator. There was no one to talk to as I waited for Linnea to return. I didn't know any of the boy-girls and girl-boys sitting around me—visiting kings and queens from Indiana, Ohio, Washington State. So I sat back and watched the girl on the stage, who didn't move well or even much at all. She only swayed back and forth, muttering along to a song about not being the right kind of woman for her man.

What kept me looking were her eyes, liquid and cocoa brown, a sad deer's downward gaze. Linnea came back with her usual scotch and handed me my usual bottle of plain water. I swigged and noticed the girl's skirt seemed to be held together with Velcro. This girl better take off her clothes or something, I whispered to Linnea, who laughed, and then, as if by my request, off came the girl's clothes.

She slipped off her blouse and rolled down the sleeves of her Harley T-shirt. She whipped off her bandana and stuffed it into the crotch of her pants and ran a square hand through her black hair, dyed rooster red along the crown, cropped nearly to the scalp above the ears. She certainly was not the right kind of woman. There she/he was, all boy oh boy, with a tough leather stance and hard rack of shoulders and all the lights back on in those pretty brown eyes. He had stepped out of the woods, arriving, in the new millennium, at the most glorious place.

Some drag is brain play, some an out-and-out flirt. Some is plain satire, but this had the bare impact of confession. Was this revelation, reinvention, or resurfacing?

There is a photograph in Diane Arbus's repertoire of Stormé DeLarverié of the Jewel Box Revue, taken in the mid-1960s, with the caption "Lady Who Appears to Be a Gentleman." Linnea and I knew of Stormé, emcee of the famous multiracial drag cabaret that toured the United States for thirty years. Linnea had even spoken to Stormé once, when we were visiting New York City, at the bar of a Chelsea restaurant with a South Beach theme, said to be Stormé's regular retirement hangout. But in the Arbus photograph Stormé was still a tenderfoot, smoking, slim-hipped, handsome, and defiant, in the way of the young butch from back in the day. The beautiful gentleman has entered the city. He wasn't letting anybody chase him away.

We were looking at the photographs with our teenage nieces, two girls from Linnea's side who have come to see us every summer for the past ten years from the cornfields of Wisconsin. Since they were small, Linnea and I have taken it upon ourselves to give the city to these girls who live on a county road, nothing to see in any direction but corn, a few homes like their own, and the requisite Walgreens. To them our little city is plenty of city. And so we take them to restaurants, feed them sushi and Pad Thai if we can find some that's not too spicy for their exurban Wisconsin palates, take them to bookstores, jazz clubs, and museums, show them abstract paintings and Ethel Merman musicals in restored movie houses screened to roomfuls of tittering gay men, show them photographs of ladies who appear to be gentlemen, point out to them—See, Stormé is just like Linnea—and then watch as they peer closer and then twitter in recognition. Ever since they were little we've wanted them to believe there is no end of possible blue yonders.

In the gallery I wandered on ahead of Linnea and the girls, then looked back to see the three of them standing before one of Arbus's photographs of circus performers. The half-man/half-woman was dressed in classic freak show drag, gender ambivalence so easily marked by a border down the center of the body—female to the right, male to the left. I looked across the gallery and saw the girls leaning toward the photograph, puzzled, unable to turn their eyes away.

These two girls are more than a little bit pretty. Their mother, Linnea's sister, is a former bathing suit model whose body used to show up, before she married our nieces' father, as a tag on department store bikinis. Even dressed down in T-shirts and tight jeans, these two are striking young women. A few nights before, at intermission in the lobby of a downtown theater, I had to restrain myself when I caught some old guy staring down the front of the fourteen-year-old's dress, even though my niece herself was still unconscious to the attentions of men in the city. Now the girls leaned into the photographs. They nudged each other, whispered into each other's ears and pointed. What was this? How should they understand it? What else had they never heard of before?

Linnea leaned toward them in the corner of the gallery, dressed much the same as they were in jeans and a T-shirt, but without the curves, without the exposed midriff and hair pulled up to the top of the head and cascading fountain-like around the ears. Linnea's hair was cropped short as Stormé's, the rectangular lenses of her heavy black eyeglasses giving her the look of a hip NASA engineer. She was standing before the bifurcated portrait gesturing like a sign-language interpreter. With one palm she marked a split down the center of her body, then pulled her hand to the right, and did the same with her left hand. Her lips were moving, and although I couldn't hear what she was saying I could imagine her patient teacher's voice explaining that no, of course that person's body was not actually split down the middle, that this was a common circus costume, that it meant to convey an idea that's harder to see, a body that doesn't fit into easy categories, an identity that has obscure borders and is neither one thing nor another, that people find such things weird and frightening and so pay good money to have a look, that this is what the photographer wants us to see, the people who don't fit, the people we don't look at hard enough or long enough, the people who make up the city we mean to give these girls, until they are grown and can find it for themselves.

Most of the kings Linnea and I saw at the Drag King Conference were not of Linnea's and my generation. Take the crowd favorite, an act I call Pretend Eminem, a cropped-haired young woman in baggy pants lip-synching to an Eminem rap. My first thought: How can a lesbian pretend to be Eminem? He's a woman hater. He's a queer basher, or at least that's what I've heard on NPR. Meanwhile sex throbbed in pretend Eminem's forearms and hard frown and all along the tense muscles of his neck. Sex throbbed through the flow, words I didn't recognize, though all the twenty-something lesbians did. When a Muslim girl in a university sweat shirt and a crisp white head cloth slipped him a dollar and kissed him on the lips, I watched all my stereotypes mutate and a new world emerge in radical dyke drag. It was not Eminem himself that mattered here, but rather this girl/boy's dream of possessing Eminem's stage power, which in the process turned the actual Eminem inside out, his rewritten illumination triggering fans to raise their arms into the air in a kind of prayer, reminding me of all the ways change is holy to the young.

American youth is for wandering dim-lit streets, for reaching up to a stage, a dollar bill gripped between the knuckles, homage to a dance of gender and sex, to the certainty that anything is possible. There is no Emerald City casting a green glow over the poppy fields. Miss Diana Ross does not sway and wave her arms around in the center of Franklin Avenue; in fact, if she's like most who see the little middle cities as flyover sectors, she probably doesn't even know where to find Minneapolis on the map. Miss Sally Bowles does not walk across predawn Minneapolis, thinking it's breakfast she's after when her real desire is to simply feel herself lifted, feel her back arc like a comma, feel the soft light of the blue city light up her face.

I don't know about Scottt, if he stayed in our little city or moved away, if he survived the 1980s, AIDS, all those older men. I don't know what happened to Leonard either, if the woman he married after I left him stayed with him, if the booze got him, or has him still, or if, like me, he doesn't drink anymore. Our cities are double cities. The city itself. The possible city. The in-between is where I finally want to live, where the practical and the projected bend like the Mississippi on a windy blue day.

The skyline of Minneapolis is actually blue. One of my favorite views of downtown, and Linnea's too, is what's visible from the Lake Street Bridge as we drive west from Saint Paul, toward our home. As we hover over the cerulean zipper of the Mississippi, the city is a small mountain range of blue and amber glass. I've read that humans didn't always consider even actual mountain ranges a thing of beauty. Some called them earth warts, as if they were eruptions marring the flat sleep of the real. It's the same with skylines. They possess only the beauty the human eye bestows.

Look, honey, our city, Linnea always says to me, as we cross over, turn to the north to see the old blue throb of the IDS, still glimmering at the center, the breadth of the skyline forever widening, making itself new. If the sun is setting, pink and yellow, light sparks off the glass. The rest of the city is still here too, the boarded-up houses of disregarded neighborhoods. Twenty-five years after I first arrived in Minneapolis, this is no longer a little city, but neither is it a megacity, nor a city of dreams. It's just a midsize midwestern city, a twin city with a river splitting the urban body in two. A long-time local once described Saint Paul to me as the last city of the East, and Minneapolis the first city of the West, which would make the Mississippi the demarcation of American change, the Old Country of my family to the right, the new country of my body, of Linnea's body, to the left.

Look at our city, Linnea says, and she does not mean a body split down the center, does not mean our youth, before us or behind us. All she means is this is the city where we live. I touch the extended muscle of Linnea's leg as she presses the gas pedal. At the center of the horizon we still see a wild gush of blue.

FIG. 12. Sanborn fire insurance map of the Trumbull Park Homes, 1947.

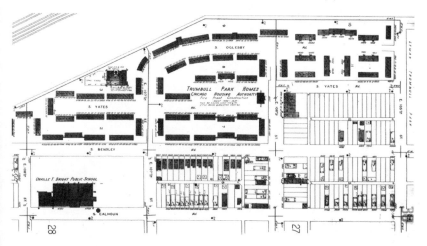

We often drove by my mother's old Trumbull Park
Homes, yet from her stories they'd seemed more legend
than history, so I was surprised to find a map.

MAP 5

When We Were in the Projects
A topography of my mother's and my Chicago

The first day of my visit with my mother in Florida, she comes home from Walmart with a brand new electric coffee percolator.

Why a percolator? Ever since the first Mr. Coffee came out in the 1970s, when I was in high school, Mom's had a drip coffeemaker. I've admired the one she's used for the past few years, sitting on the counter in her kitchen overlooking the golf course. It's the kind with a thermal pot, the type that keeps the coffee warm without burning it up.

But today Mom's come home with a percolator, and now she's fiddling with it, complaining about all the things it won't do. It doesn't have a timer, she says. I can't set it up the night before. It doesn't have instructions. Can I use my regular coffee?

I ask her, Why did you buy it? I'm the child who worries her by not trying hard enough to own all the right appliances. She'll buy me the televisions or electric can openers she's sure I need, whether or not I want them. But when it comes to her own home, she thinks before she spends. She's frugal to the point of haranguing my dad if he buys a book. The percolator, though, was an impulse purchase. She just saw it and picked it up. She didn't even read the box. She always used to have percolators. She remembers the coffee was good.

Inset of the Projects

For my mother, the kinds of appliances she has in her kitchen, the kind of house she lives in, the size of the television she watches, and the features of the car she drives are all responses to her childhood spent in the Projects. Her Projects were in South Deering, also called Irondale or Slag Valley, on the far South Side of Chicago, a few blocks from the old Wisconsin Steel plant. Her Projects are to me like a 3D slide of Graceland, or the bleak setting of an English novel, or any of the old-time Chicago world's fairs—places I've never visited but feel as if I know because I've heard so much about them.

My brothers and I grew up within my mother's mantras, the countless sentences that begin *When we were in the Projects*. When Little Grandma Luschak finally moved out of the Projects, she relocated only a couple blocks away. My mother always pointed out the Projects when we drove past, on the way to or from her mother's apartment, but all I could see were yellow brick buildings laid out like train cars, just two stories high, with flat roofs and teensy lawns. The Trumbull Park Homes, built before the infamous towers farther north and closer to the lake, were the old style of Chicago projects, originally designed for steelworkers, mostly Croats, Serbs, Poles, and Italians back then, row houses clustered around a bland courtyard. It wasn't just my mother who called them the Projects. Nobody in the neighborhood called them the Trumbull Park Homes. The Projects were their proper name, pronounced with a hard capital *P*. *Your father used to pick me up for dates in the Projects*, my mother always says. *In the Projects I used to scrub the walls until my hands turned red.*

In the 1950s, when my mother lived in the Projects, they were not quite the forgotten spaces of today's inner cities. Still, my mother talks about them the way veterans talk about battlefields, the way hurricane survivors talk about the big waves. The Projects were her disaster, her big war, her burning house. She still smells the scent of smoke on her skin.

Inset of the Percolator

Recently I spotted a red 1960s percolator with gold starbursts, set on a high shelf of an antique store. Right away I wanted it, even imagined it in my kitchen surrounded by our Fiestaware dishes and red vinyl chairs, perking away—dare I say perkily? It would match the red diner-style kitchen table Linnea bought at some poor slob's get-out-of-town-quick garage sale, across the alley from the duplex where we lived our first ten years together. But I didn't ask the sales clerk to pull the red perker down for me. Linnea and I already own both a French press and an espresso machine, not to mention the stovetop percolator Linnea takes out when a retro coffee mood strikes. I don't need a red percolator.

Linnea and I are attracted to older styles of design. On our very first date, dinner in my south Minneapolis studio apartment, one of us commented that the type of furniture we loved best was Art Deco, and the other one of us, I no longer remember which, whispered, Me too. It was our first mutual turn-on. The next thing we knew, we were stretched out on my couch, kissing. The couch was a 1950s wagon-wheel foldout I picked up for $100 in a local used furniture store, the first big piece of furniture I'd ever bought, made of turquoise Naugahyde. It had a saddle imprinted into the back cushion, wheels built into the sides. It was the sort of couch you see in movies about women who went west to Reno in the 1940s and '50s to wait for a divorce. So Linnea and I fell in love in the 1980s on a Reno divorce couch, just before the mid-twentieth century qualified as antique. That's when they began, Linnea's and my collections of items that could have been in our parents' apartments the year we were born.

Inset of the Prairie

I still lived with my mother the last time she used a percolator. That would have been in the old house at 14200 Emerald. This brings me to the smoke that I still smell on my skin—not actual smoke, but a smoky shadow, a sheath of the past that perhaps I could shed if I wanted to. Instead I work to preserve it, keep it like a historical souvenir, a long dead spider perpetually crouched in an amber haze, frozen but still visible, suspended and unable to sting.

Across the alley behind our house was Halsted Avenue, always busy, always rattling with semitrailers driving down from the South Side mills and warehouses of the city. Across the street was an open tract of land we called the Prairie. We called any empty lot in Chicago a prairie. It was one of those words nobody thought about but everyone spoke. Now I see how poorly the word fits that weedy stretch, bordered by train tracks and truck routes and the brick bungalows of the working-class suburbs and canopied by the giant steel frames of high-tension wires. That was no prairie. It was open ground, an undeveloped industrial patch too close to the wires to make room for homes or stores. Now I know what a prairie really is. The tall grass that stoops in the wind. The green sea of inland America, swallowed by the plow. That semi-open space across the street from 14200 Emerald was no prairie.

But then again it was the prairie, or had been once. All of Illinois was once tallgrass prairie. The first outsider settlers, French priests trading with the Pottawatomie, had to part the grass with their arms and knees before shaking hands or smoking the pipe called the calumet with indigenous locals who would soon become history. That's what our industrial stink plain was named, long before I was born. Calumet. The prairie land that turned into a rail yard, a slag heap, and little brown brick houses with percolators pumping perkily on Formica countertops while the black-and-white televisions flickered with newscasters intoning through a cigarette mist or with the perky smiles and pointed training bras of the Disney Mousketeers.

Across the street from the house on Emerald Avenue, in the center of our prairie, sat an abandoned grain mill, the Hales & Hunter grain elevator. If I pressed my cheek against the glass and craned my neck I could see it from my bedroom window. The South Side of Chicago in the early 1970s was full of forsaken factories and mills. We took school field trips to the Wonder Bread factory and the Museum of Science and Industry, but no one ever mentioned the plethora of dead warehouses and broken-down manufacturing plants. Whatever wreckage we couldn't see from our yard, we drove past on the way to Little Grandma's apartment in the old neighborhood.

The kids in the blocks around our house called that old grain mill the Rat Factory. The umber walls were smeared with graffiti, the windows punched out. If the square-shouldered Rat Factory had a face, it looked as if birds had pecked out its eyes. When we kids, walking home from school, got too close to Rat Factory—by this point Rat Factory had become a proper name—we hunched over to make ourselves smaller. We slowed our steps and shrank our voices to a whisper. Our lunchboxes banged against each other's elbows. As we got closer to 142nd Street, Rat Factory stood up on its haunches. What would it do? Suck us in? Swallow us whole? Grind us into flour and feed us to the rats? We ran, cutting across the grass of the corner houses, screaming and barreling west toward Emerald Avenue, two blocks, one block more. Emerald Avenue beckoned like the lights of Emerald City as Rat Factory retreated into the background, settling back into its prairie bed.

The first pot of coffee my mother makes with her new Florida percolator is pale brown. Coffee that's too weak has a dirty taste. I can't drink it. My mother, on the other hand, is happy with supermarket coffee that comes in a vacuum-packed can. She's suspicious of the beans that cost ten bucks a bag and is leery of the grinders set up in the coffee aisle for the people who don't have grinders at home. So I'm surprised she's making such a fuss over this percolator. Mom, I ask her, why don't you just use your old pot? You used that pot just fine for years now. No, I didn't, she says. That pot's terrible. It's supposed to keep the coffee warm, but the coffee gets cold anyway. And I keep setting up the timer and forgetting to put the carafe in. What a mess, all over my counter.

That sounds like operator error, Mom, I tell her.

Inset of the Projects

Even though I've always known that my mother's Projects really exist, I'm not sure I really believed it as a kid. No, *believe* is not the right word. I believed, but that belief wasn't physical, not the way our actual house with its brown bricks and prickly hedge and heavy basement door with the wooden barricade instead of a lock was physical. The Projects were a faded movie, the kind that burns up when it gets too close to the projector bulb. I couldn't imagine actually walking through the Projects. The past was not a country my parents returned to. No guided tour. No packet of historical data. The past was a place you leave, a place to forget, a place to change away from, to pile up on the curb until the truck comes to take it away.

I imagine the walls of the Projects were bare but clean, because my mother told me how often she scrubbed, until her elbows hurt and her knuckles were raw. I don't see how those walls could have been dirty enough to need all that scrubbing. It must have been a feeling my mother was trying to scrape away, the shadow of the mill smoke, so thick it could have been meringue, except it was too gray to be like meringue and the eggs had gone bad, and there is no stink like eggs gone bad. She wanted to scrub all of it away, the coppery slag pilings, refuse from the mills that looked like pyres of collapsed bones, the sanitary district where her father worked, the whole stinking toilet-scape of the far Southeast Side. The memory of smell is almost all it takes to re-create that smell; she can't ever get rid of it completely, just like she can't scrub away the odor of cigarettes and whiskey that wafted out of her father's pores, even though he's been dead since I was a freshman in college.

And too I think my mother must have been scrubbing away at her certainty that there might never be enough, that it might all go down under her, that she'd sooner or later have nothing left, nowhere to sleep, nothing solid against her skin, nothing pretty or valuable to call her own. It's the pull to rise out of the urban underclass that motivated her every move, no looking back at the pile-up of people lining up behind, the ones looking forward to moving into the same space she wished so badly to abandon.

When I visit Florida we go to a restaurant near my parents' retirement house, the nice fish place down the road, the one where muscular gay men who work out at the same gym as my father have replaced the old lady waitresses with high hair and cigarette-crossed voices. We don't eat the rolls, so my mother asks the waiter if he will wrap them up to go. They're just rolls. Just half rolls, some of them, the ones I'd picked at, pretending I wasn't eating the bread. Not worth saving. But Mom will not leave uneaten food on the table. One of us—her kids who try to fill her in on all the ways the world has progressed since she lived in the Projects—must have told her to ask the waiter for a bag; she used to just dump the rolls into her purse when the server's back was turned.

Mom, I'd say, why do you need those rolls? You've *retired* in *Florida*. This isn't the *Projects* anymore. Outside the restaurant window, the dock water glistens. Boats rock against the docks, the swooshing barely audible through the glass. No, this is nothing like the Projects. Mom, you can afford to buy rolls, I'd say. Why should I pay for new rolls? she'd say. I'm already paying for these rolls. The waiter brings back our half-eaten rolls in a Styrofoam box. Mom wraps up the conversation the same way every time. *You'll never get the Projects out of me*, she says.

Inset of My Collections

Every time Linnea and I clean out our cabinets for a yard sale, we realize we might have trouble letting go of the past. I make fun of the way my mother moved half of Chicago into her wooden A-frame in Florida, but I'm no better. I forget that it's not actual memory that collectors save, just objects that look like memory.

Such is my collection of mid-twentieth-century TV lamps. I have more than twenty of them now—pairs of poodles and birds of paradise, lilies and leaping gazelles, an abstract cluster of leaves that look like a head of lettuce, and even a ceramic fireplace made with translucent clay, my collection incomplete until I find that ceramic light-up accordion. They are my favorite things, silly ceramic statuary, sold in the 1950s to set on top of the TV, a hood ornament for then-new TV consoles, modern and practical, and promising to reduce TV-tube eyestrain. TV lamps, along with atomic curtain fabric design and anything that pictured a poodle, were part of the twentieth-century, mid-industrial-era, American domesticity fetish. Finally, a nice house. In a clean neighborhood with lawns and freestanding houses. Finally, we are out of the Projects.

Linnea broke one of my lamps recently, while moving the furniture to plug in the digital TV connection. Honey, I said, be careful of my TV lamps. Yeah yeah, she said, and a few moments later I heard a crash. When I saw the broken ceramic birds, no longer poised for flight above a porcelain planter, I cried, as if I'd lost something that mattered, something crucial and imprecise as memory itself.

Linnea glued the birds back together. I can't see the cracks unless I look closely. Still, I don't know what I'm doing, gathering up these objects, more things to dust. It may be enough to just say I like them, that they are silly and useless and make me laugh, but I suspect they are more. I tell myself I collect to stay aware of all these layers, all this archiving, but it could be I prefer a kitschy history, the kind I can control.

My mother is frustrated with her new percolator. She can't control it. The coffee doesn't taste like she remembers percolated coffee tasting. She asks me, Am I doing this wrong? She asks me, Doesn't Linnea have a percolator? What does she do to make her coffee so good? Linnea does have a percolator, the type that sits on the stove and shoots coffee up into its glass-knobbed lid. And Linnea makes good coffee. But she has the kitchen thumb. It's not fair to compare. When my parents come to visit, she makes them coffee in that percolator because it looks more like a coffee pot to them than the press pot or espresso machine we'd otherwise use.

So I call Linnea and tell her, Mom wants your advice on using her new percolator. Well, Linnea says, first be sure the coffee cooks long enough. It takes longer than the Mr. Coffee. Oh, my mother says, and frowns. This is not good news. She doesn't want it to take longer. She just wants it to taste better. And stay warmer. She wants to make it at 6 a.m. when she gets up, and she wants it to stay warm until 11 a.m., when she pours another cup. She wants a lot, I almost point out, but then don't bother. I might not be able to help her with this percolator problem.

Then tell her, Linnea continues, that my grandmother used to toss in eggshells. Eggshells? I ask her. What does that do? I don't know, Linnea says. It's some old Italian thing. So I tell her, Mom, Linnea says her grandmother throws in eggshells. Eggshells? my mother asks. Do I have to wash them off first? No, no, I tell her, just save the shells and put them in with the coffee grounds. Well, I'm not going to waste an egg just for the coffee, Mom says.

Inset of the Home Movie

Before my parents moved to Florida I absconded with two collections: my dad's battered old jazz albums and the dusty reels of home movies that no one had looked at for years, ever since Dad's old projector finally broke down. A year or so later was when I pulled that box of film out from the closet under my stairs and rented a projector. The film flickered against the white paper screen, the film images harder and crisper than they'd look later, once I had them transferred to videotape. I watched those scenes from the day my mother brought me home from the hospital, swaddled in her arms, and scenes of one of my birthday parties, a swarm of children playing London Bridge on the front lawn, and then the scenes that really surprised me, footage of the Projects. My mother's middle brother, the one who used to look like Elvis, sat in an upstairs window and waved. My other uncle, a skinny teenager who would later work on his Edsel collection in our garage, opened the front door and beckoned us in.

When I saw that footage I shivered. It was as if a story had trans-mogrified into a hologram, as if language had become a body. The buildings were not remarkable. Plain brick, windows square and open. My Elvis uncle was younger and more relaxed than he seemed to me later, when I actually knew him, living in a messy back room of his mother's apartment. No, the difference was this: My mother's mantra became a body of space, the province of her constant and repetitive storytelling, the place her whole life has been dedicated to leaving, but also a geography that exists without her, in real time, in history. I couldn't tell if this made the Projects less of a story, or more.

When is a prairie a plot of industrial detritus, and when is it a sea of wild grass? When is a percolator an item of nostalgia in an antique shop specializing in overflow from mid-twentieth-century American kitchens, and when is it the best way to make coffee? The percolator is a cliché for bubbling over, for fresh, fast, and new ways of thinking, but the coffee my mother makes in her new Walmart percolator just doesn't taste that good.

Linnea says maybe my mother bought that percolator so she could make coffee for me. She comes to our house, Linnea says, and our coffee is different from hers, not regular coffee. Maybe to her the percolator seems fancier. Maybe she's just trying to make coffee that you'll drink. At first I say, No no, that's not it. She told me she didn't know why she bought it; she just saw it and placed it in her shopping cart without thinking. But the minute I say it I take it back. My mother has always told me she doesn't believe in psychological reasons for things, so if I asked she would pooh-pooh the idea. But the more I think about it the more I see Linnea's point.

Back in the 1960s, when Mom replaced her old percolator with a Mr. Coffee, she had stepped into an ever-cleaner world. Fill the paper basket with coffee. Pour the water in at the back. Push the button, and the coffee drips out into a clear glass carafe. The dirty grounds never stick in the basket holes, never touch her hands.

Nostalgia is the past with the messy grounds removed, nothing but the surface remaining. Those 1950s ads of well-groomed housewives with starry smiles serving dinner in crisp yellow dresses and comfortable heels are funny to us now, but back then they were a promise. So my mother is wheeling her way through Walmart the day her only daughter is coming to visit, the kid who turned out so different, who likes that fancy strong coffee, and she sees the image of a gleaming percolator on the box and remembers when the perky fountain of coffee sitting on her kitchen counter was the picture of her escape. The percolator was fancy; that's what she remembers.

If that's true, then she must be disappointed when I set on her counter the Italian Roast that I'd carried all the way from Minneapolis and proceed to make coffee in my new toy, a silver mug with a press pot plunger built right in. I show the French press cup to Mom, demonstrate how it works. That's pretty fancy, my mother says.

Inset of the Prairie

People I've told in my adulthood about Rat Factory have imagined a pinched-face, stoop-shouldered gangster called Ratty, ugly enough, but too small. I don't always remember to mention that our Rat Factory was as tall as a ten-story office building, and wide as well, the width of four or five of our houses.

Truman Capote once described midwestern grain elevators as Greek temples, but he was writing about Kansas, towers rising out of a wide swath of open farmland. Rat Factory, more pyramid then temple, had brick neighborhoods and train tracks and electrical lines huddled around it from all sides. Most of the time we sensed it more than saw it, the way we were aware of tornados and presidential assassins, real enough on the nightly news, but not the kind of thing you want to look in the face.

According to neighborhood stories, there really were rats inside Rat Factory, although I never saw them. All grain mills had rats, because in a grain mill there is plenty for rats to eat. In the 1960s, before we lived there, Rat Factory caught fire, causing the rats to run for their lives. An army of rats fled the mill, filing into the prairie, crossing 142nd Street, burrowing into the basements of the homes in the streets surrounding.

Rats or no rats, Emerald Avenue, while fancier than the Projects, was not nearly fancy enough from my mother's point of view. Yet today when I type that old address, 14200 Emerald, into an Internet street atlas, what comes up on my computer screen is simply a pale yellow map, not Rat Factory, not even a palette of my mother's fears, those invisible perpetrators she named *unsavory characters*, hiding like rats in the broken prairie brush. A red star marks where our old house stands, at the corner of a tight grid of streets that cup the bottom of the city. Emerald Avenue was a block of boxy houses, evenly spaced. The lawns were square and the chain-link fences hemmed us all in neatly. I might remember the name of the avenue, not as I knew it but as it sounds, green and cradling an inner flicker, or I might remember it as it was, not a gem, just a residential street a few blocks beyond the mill smoke, or I might remember all of it at once. The abandoned prospects of the post-steel American metropolis. The fear of rats that may not have been actual rats but only my mother's unspoken shadows, not just her father's poverty but also his fumbling whiskey hands. I might remember the actual avenue and also the promise of some fancier city, awaiting both her and my escape.

My mother had a dishwasher in the Emerald Avenue house, not the built-in kind she has now, but the kind with wheels. My dad, a member of the camera club, built a darkroom in the basement. The weeping willow in the yard fingered its way into the foundation, the flowering bushes in the yard popped into bloom each spring and shook showers of pink petals across the grass, and in the garage my uncle sanded and painted and resanded and repainted another old car. Once I squeezed into the dome-like front seat of his latest Edsel with one of my brothers, and my uncle drove us along the perimeter of the prairie, safe inside the steel skin tank of the car, while the prairie weeds billowed and Rat Factory glowered but couldn't get near us. Back home my mother set a cup of percolated coffee on the yellow speckled counter and forgot about it until it was too cold to drink.

FIG. 13. The Rat Factory. Hales & Hunter Feed Mill, Riverdale, Illinois.

A prairie is a fancy plain of grass, diverse and spectacular, billowing like the sea. A prairie is an industrial dump with wire-laced skies and rat-faced factories. The Projects were supposed to be planned communities, orchestrated fanciness, a shelter, a nice clean place to live for people who worked hard for their money, but they turned out to be, for my mother at least, a purgatory. The memories we collect are the smiley faces and uncracked hearts, pressed like pretty leaves between the pages of the dictionary. The memories that stick without our efforts have dirty walls and rat-infested basements. *When we were in the Projects*, my mother begins. She means not just then but also now.

I will never ask my mother if she finally does what she's been threatening to do the whole week of my visit, which is to clean up that percolator, put it back in the box, and return it to Walmart. I won't get involved in her arguments with Dad about whether it's too late, now that she's used it. Dad and I both know if she wants to take it back, she will.

But if what Mom really wants is to make me a cup of coffee fancier than the Projects, then we are at an impasse. She reaches for the percolator at Walmart because the fancy picture on the box reminds her less of coffee than of her old longing to leave. I long for the percolator at the antique store because I love the funniness of the lie, the snazzy starburst design and the swanky spout, the promise of a perkier-than-possible future. My mother's and my ideas of fancy meet, then part again.

Before I leave Florida I try to brew a pot of my dark Italian Roast in Mom's percolator. I'd like to say that this is the winning equation: the daughter's content plus the mother's technology equal a fancy cup of coffee we can both enjoy. But my coffee is ground too coarsely, meant for the press pot. It clogs the works of my mother's percolator. Neither of us can drink it. We leave the cups of grainy black brew on her counter until the golfers outside her kitchen window, retirees from the northern mill cities or midwestern suburbs or the southern air force bases, drive their carts back to their two-car garage arcadias, the course turning blue under the setting sun, the coffee cold.

FIG. 14. *My Father Wanders* by Robert A. Borich, 1969.

What then is a daughter to do with the gift of her father's map?

MAP 6

Navigating Jazz
A map to the end of longing, with insets
of my father's and my escape

Inset of Legend and Contour

Miss Nancy Wilson is wearing a lemon yellow dress. The dress is what I remember, from the album jacket, Fancy Miss Nancy, jazz song stylist, the thrush from Columbus. First her tight yellow dress, then Miss Nancy herself, one arm flung into the air, her mouth open. She's singing. Filling that dress up with her breath. Cannonball Adderley laughs in the background, holding onto his horn as if it were about to fly away by the force of its own sound. Cannonball and Miss Nancy are having a hell of a time.

The album was my dad's, part of the collection I used to flip through as a girl, making slow progress on dusting, one of my teenage chores, which I took as an opportunity to rummage through things that didn't belong to me.

Once I found my mom and dad's old love letters in the back of a bedroom dresser. Another time I found my mother's diaphragm, shoved into the back of the linen closet, abandoned, I can only presume, when she came to terms, as a Catholic woman, with taking the pill. And I found my dad's photography books, not hidden, in plain view on a living-room shelf. Alone, with the dust rag bunched up in my lap, I paged through to Annie Leibovitz's portrait of Lily Tomlin wearing a halter top, her head obscured by a television screen broadcasting an image of her face. The caption under the photo tantalizingly referred to Lily as bisexual. I returned to it often.

My mother's copy of *Judy Garland at Carnegie Hall*, a double-album set, drew me as well. This was the vinyl 1960s, and Judy was my favorite TV variety-show very special guest. I loved the way her torso twisted with the movement of a song, her gaunt face and tipsy smile, her messy bedroom hair. These days when I see film clips of 1960s Judy I notice her weave and stutter and understand she might have been drunk, but back then I loved the way she seemed to tremble under her clothes.

As a grown woman I know now what I couldn't understand then, that my finds—from love letters to pictures of women flinging and gesticulating—were all about sound and sex and escape, coordinates on an awkward teenage girl's still nebulous map of longing.

My dad says to his mother: I was a bad kid.

I am in Florida, in the development Bay Point, where my parents and my grandmother retired, my annual January visit, sitting with Dad in the dreamy dusk of Gram's kitchen, where she pretends she can still see me. Gram Rose tells me I look good, that I haven't changed a bit, as if I were still a leggy girl with long strings of naturally blond hair, not an eccentrically dressed adult woman. My boots, dyed hair, and arty eyeglasses blend in up north, in the cities, but I stick out down here among the snowbirds and beach retirees, and I'm hardly a teenager.

The blinds in this kitchen are closed tight. None of us can see the grass canal of the golf course. Gram covers the windows to keep the man from next door from looking in. That's what she says, that the man from next door watches her. All the time. She has to keep the blinds shut tight.

And Gram does not agree with my father's proclamation. You were always such a good guy, she says to Dad, as she eats the salad he made for her, the same salad he makes every night, between 5:30 and 5:45, just before he heats up her Meals-on-Wheels dinner and sets up her coffee pot for the next morning. Green lettuce. Blue cheese dressing. This is delicious, Gram says, and she means it, licking the dressing off her lips. She needs strong tastes now to know what she's eating: blue cheese dressing, coconut shrimp, ketchup.

I've noticed, with each visit to Florida, Gram's gradual decline, but this is the first time I've seen my dad with a routine. Gram Duty, my mother calls it. It goes something like this. My white-haired, golf-course-tanned father enters through the garage, which he opens with the garage door opener he keeps in his car. When he walks in he shouts as loud as he can, because Gram, the former nurse who once kept track of all the implements and pills of a downtown Chicago doctor's office, has lost her hearing aid again. *Mother*, he shouts, *Mother*, but she doesn't always hear. The television is blaring, someone on Fox News is shouting. Someone on Fox News is always shouting. Sometimes Gram, her once meticulous white topknot askew, sits staring toward the talking shadows of a television she can't quite see.

Mother, my dad shouts, and sooner or later she'll hear something and jerk for a moment, before she covers, pretends she's not surprised, pretends she's fully conscious, that she can see us. When I visit I tag along on Gram Duty and do my small part. If she's sitting I lean over her, touch her elbow. *Gram*, I shout. Sometimes it takes a minute before she knows me. Sometimes it takes a minute before she knows my father is my father, and not my cousin Antony, who also lives in this golf course compound, who also visits Gram, but not every day and never to make her salad with blue cheese dressing. Antony is louder, broader, burlier than Dad, and my age, middle-forties, the age range within which Gram prefers to remember her son.

On this day, when we get there, Gram is in her kitchen, peering through an opening in her back shade, her stiff white hair fallen loose around her face, as if she's been up all night on a stakeout. I ask my dad, What's she looking at? I know he understands the nuance of my question. She can't see, so what could she be looking at? My dad shrugs. The man next door?

I ask, Why does she think he's watching her? Is he out there working on his house? Dad shakes his head. No. No. The guy's at work all day. He doesn't watch her. *Mother,* he shouts. *Mother. We're here.*

Inset of My Father Navigating Jazz

My parents' love letters were stored so casually, as if Mom hadn't noticed that she had children who could read. The paper was light green with lines of a darker green. The letters nestled in their original envelopes, tied together with a thread. They rustled when I pulled them out of their skins. I picture Mom as she looked then, what I know from old snapshots, wearing sleek plaid Capri pants, her bleached blond hair pulled off her face with a ribbon, writing to her husband, who is away, in the army, about their recent wedding night. And I picture Dad, still a football player, stiff in his hard wooden army desk chair, writing his new wife letters about jazz.

The last time I was in Florida Gram Rose was still able to let me take her out to lunch. I drove her down the desolate January beach, found an open restaurant, ordered coconut shrimp, which she swore was the best thing she had ever tasted, ever, in her whole life, and she'd been all over the world, did I know?

When I got back to my parents' house, Dad was alone, upstairs, working at his computer. The light within the polished wooden walls was gold, contained. It shouldn't surprise me anymore that their vacation home has become their real home, that they actually live in Florida now, not in Chicago but in this house, where the walls of the upstairs rooms don't reach all the way to the ceiling, so every sound from every corner of the house—my mother's TV talk shows, my dad's jazz, the water pump on the turtle tank—is audible at all times, where every doll and statue, book and polished piece of driftwood I remember from childhood is crammed into what seems no more than half the space of the home where I grew up.

My dad had his bebop ramped up high and the light from his computer screen was the brightest light in the room. I didn't know what he'd been working on, probably the Gulf Coast Jazz Society newsletter, but I could tell he'd been in a groove. Still, he stopped when I came in, asked me, How do you think she is?

Worse, I said. I reported how she kept repeating things, even more than she used to.

Dad nodded. Was he as sad as he looked, or were those naturally down-turned lips and moody eyes a family trait, another old Croatian expression I've inherited? Sometimes people think I'm sad, or even angry, when I'm nothing, just neutral. If I'd asked my dad then if he was sad he would have tsk-tsked me. He was never sad, he'd say. But he looked sad when he talked about Gram. My mother was a cold woman, he said. I never felt encouraged by her.

This was more than Dad had ever told me about his mother. I was silent, wanting to prolong this unexpected story, but I'd had no practice at trading intimacies with my father.

Dad has always enjoyed discussing what lies hidden beneath the surface. He's where I get my own propensity to ruminate. When high school friends used to tell me I was deep, it was not always a compliment. Deep might be interesting once in a while, but it was also boring, unfun, a waste of time.

But being deep is not what makes us our parents' bad children. I might be a bad daughter, but my dad is not a bad son. He never moved away from his mother. Never refused to come home for Christmas. Never migrated away into a life that might not include her.

Still, when my father was a young man, he did let himself get deep, and while he was under, in the depths, his private Village Vanguard, he found loose spaces that were different from his mother's cool ordered city where she knew how to dance up a storm.

Inset of Legend and Contour (Alternate View)

The jacket of that Nancy Wilson album might be the legend I use to read the map of my father. Here's a guy who grows up on the then still all-white Southeast Side of Chicago, the son of an unapproachable mother and an immigrant father who died in his sleep, before his oldest child became a man. Here's a guy who raises his kids in the still-segregated steel mill suburbs of the 1960s, on a street where neighbors used to stop his daughter on her way home from school to ask, not in a friendly way, were we thinking of *selling to blacks*? Here's a guy who never left his family and yet does depart daily, when he migrates into jazz.

But that album jacket I think I remember so clearly—when I buy it, as an adult, on CD, I see I've remembered the image all wrong. Nancy Wilson and Cannonball Adderley are indeed on the cover, but nobody is gesticulating or laughing. Miss Nancy is wearing that yellow dress, though, and I see why I remember it. The dress is sleeveless, with an hourglass fit over the waist, hips, and thighs, the neckline deep but not plunging, not revealing so much as suggesting. Her yellow high-heeled pumps are dyed to match, so that the deep yellow, hot yellow, pop art lemon yellow blasts off against her caramel brown skin.

I've always loved the way women look in 1960s cocktail dresses, and still do. These were dresses singers wore on *The Ed Sullivan Show*, the dresses my fancy Auntie Lucy wore in snapshots of dinner dates with her fiancé, the laughing salesman. Nancy Wilson smiles over her shoulder, at Cannon (as he is called on the liner notes), who wears a slick black suit, the sax in his hands as golden as Nancy's dress is yellow. Nancy's dark hair is rounded and puffed, the same way my mother wore her hair in the 1960s. Cannon's expression is unreadable, but I imagine he could be thinking something like, *Baby*, you are so *fine* I havta play you a *tune*. Nancy's arms are crossed over her chest. I'm obviously gorgeous, her posture says, but don't you get too close.

I doubt it's an accident that Nancy Wilson's record promoters put her in a sexy yellow cocktail dress in order to sell platters to guys like my father, guys who went deeper than they ever had before the first time they listened to jazz. The promoters knew how to lure young white guys out of the realms of their coolly assimilated white ethnic mothers. Miss Nancy wears her dress, and her hair, just the way Mrs.

Laura Petrie might have on *The Dick Van Dyke Show*. The liner notes discuss her as a singer, not a black woman, praising her phrasing, tone, and control. But those same album notes reveal something else. The jazz critic describes Miss Wilson's singing as alternately "delicate and savage." The promotions department means for the potential fan to see both her sex and her skin, but a version skewed by a white racist map denoting a black woman's body, a black woman's voice, as something the white listener could be expected to both love and long to civilize, meaning my father's freedom, even if well-meaning, might have contributed to Miss Nancy Wilson's captivity.

I don't know if my dad responded to things like tight dresses and smiles tossed over the shoulder, don't know if he would have been vulnerable to the commercial manipulation of race and sex and the early civil rights–era razor's edge of the breakthrough of African American artists, but then who wouldn't have been? Still, I doubt he bought the album for the dress. Not only for the dress.

Inset of Body Tectonics (Convergent)

Let's say my dad is not a bad son, that I am not a bad daughter, but that like my dad, more so than my dad, I did leave my family, chasing whatever I sought in Lily's halter top, in Judy's hopped-up jazz arms, in the cleavage revealed by Fancy Miss Nancy's dress. Let's say that's where I live now, in the tectonic plate between so many migrations, when I sit with Linnea at our red kitchen table talking, the way we do.

When we go out Linnea dresses like a cool-cat gentleman who might have frequented the 1950s Village Vanguard, but at home, on a winter Saturday, in her sweat pants and knit Bears cap, she could be any age, any gender. It is my custom, as we sit, to barrage her with questions. Such as, Why do you think poodle kitsch goes for such high prices on eBay? Such as, Why do you think Gram believes the man next door is watching her? Such as, What do you notice, on this album cover, about Nancy Wilson's dress?

Linnea is usually happy to take a run at my questions, whether or not she knows the answers, even if she'd rather be watching the Bears game, playing right now, on the small TV on the kitchen counter just behind our heads. The windows are not well insulated, and it's below zero outside, so the glass surrounding the kitchen is tinged with frost. Linnea is still a Chicago Bears fan, even after twenty years in Vikings territory. She sneaks a peek over one shoulder at the game. Poodle nostalgia, she says. Porcelain poodles represent the past made safe. Sundowner's Syndrome, she says. It's a form of dementia that leads old people to believe the night is watching them. And as for the dress, what she says is *Hubba hubba*.

The Nancy Wilson CD is balanced on its end, on top of several weeks' worth of unread Minneapolis and New York City newspapers. Nancy Wilson's dress is as yellow as a school bus.

I ask if there is any way to talk about this album cover without mentioning race. Don't you think it's intentional? Don't you think the PR man wanted people to notice her skin? Linnea says: Probably. The frost on the window turns the light in our kitchen smoky. Linnea says: Jazz was the first American art form created primarily by African Americans that white people gravitated toward.

So then I say: Did it change that first generation of white people like my dad when they listened to jazz? Did listening change their location? Did their listening change jazz?

Linnea says: Everything we love changes our location, and locations are always in some state of change.

I say: So what about the dress?

Linnea says: Sexy. Will you get a dress like that?

Inset of Their Broken Time

I don't recall the words Dad used in his letters to Mom. Though Dad was in the army it wasn't wartime. He was in the desert, Arizona, serving his time inside a wide orange and yellow watercolor landscape, land the same color as the jazz paintings he had hanging in our basement when I was a kid, orange saxophones and an amber guitar. I don't know where he got them, but occasionally, at estate sales, I see similar artwork. I remember those paintings as having a sound, wide and orange and dry. Like the desert at night. This was his military service, so Dad must have learned to use a gun, to march, to follow orders, but the only weapon he ever told his kids about operating was a typewriter, the old clacking kind, that he used the way the old-time journalists did, typing memos and forms fast with just his two forefingers. But his letters to Mom weren't typed. I recognized his narrow loping handwriting, so distinctive; my mother must have felt a jolt when she pulled them out of the mailbox in Chicago.

This was the 1950s, when bebop was new. This kind of jazz, my dad wrote to my mom, is not made for dancing; it's a completely new sound. The downbeat jars against what we expect, makes us over. That is at least what I think he was trying to say, that the music pushed him into his own body. So he wrote to his new wife, told her that if she listened she would hear it. The tones. Burnished orange, against a blue sky.

Inset of Body Improvisation

I know about new territories. I've lived in one myself, for nearly as long as Gram has lived in Florida. Longer. It's the way I felt that first time I fell in love with a woman. The old world receding. The new world immersing me in unfamiliar light. But that's not it exactly. I don't want to simplify. What was the gray and copper landscape of the steel mill side of Chicago, what were the druggy disco-hating art rock bacchanals of my high school party friends, what was getting high with older guys whose dads harangued them because their hair was so goddamned long—became an opposite country, impossibly fierce and cheerful women who kissed each other in public and ate brown rice and fresh vegetables and lived in windy houses lost in the Illinois corn fields.

But that's not what I mean either. To emigrate to a new territory is to tear away from everything familiar, to expose yourself, raw and without protection to another climate altogether, to have no idea what to do or say, to lose your footing, to lose the ground to place your feet. It wasn't just my emigration to the late 1970s Lesbian Nation, a very different place from where I'd come from. I used to think the first move was the whole story, coming out queer in itself the arrival. Now that seems too easy an explanation, the theme missing its improvisation. My migration wasn't made of sex with women so much as it was sex itself, but not only sex. Sex I was awake to notice. Or swimming slowly across a city lake, without a goal. Or drinking strong tea in bed, aware of each ping of the body awakening. Not so much sex as being open to sex, being open to anything that might make me over, and in the process not knowing what my presence might ruin or might refresh. The clackity clack of an old-time typewriter, jarring against what I expected. A yellow dress, cinched tight just under the breasts. A solo horn, an involuntary cry.

Gram Rose was lost on the golf course again, on her way to or from the post office, the day she met the man next door. For twenty-five years she'd walked that golf course, since the days when mostly retirees lived at Bay Point, when the signs that read "Duck Crossing" were not just duck kitsch, but signs warning drivers of actual ducks. In those days Gram walked along the edge of the course itself or down the middle of the streets; back then she wasn't taking a risk because drivers really did slow down for old ladies. But families live in the complex now. School buses rumble through, and young boys drive Daddy's car too fast, and middle-aged people speed up when they realize they're late for work.

The day the man next door picked her up, Gram was wandering. It was probably not her face that gave her away. She has always been a master at the mask. The man next door must have known she was lost by the direction she was going, or by the way the wind was whipping through her hair as she moved more and more slowly. Gram would not have asked for help.

He must have pulled up next to her. Rose, let me drive you. You know me. I live right next door. They would have made small talk. How chilly that wind was. How cold it was in November. She may have assumed his offer of a ride was more than neighborly interest. She may have even flirted with him. I'd seen her do this, even in her midnineties, her makeup caked over her forehead, wearing the same clothes she'd worn the day before. She'd bat her eyelashes. She'd told me many times, That's what men like, women who bat their eyelashes. She's the only one I've ever seen do this, aside from cartoon characters and actresses in silent movies. Her chin came up. Her head tilted. Even her spine curved a bit. She smiled as if enthralled by whatever the man had to say.

What this man said was, apparently, nothing much, just that he was a realtor, that he owned an agency called Bay Point, the same name as the complex where they all lived. What Gram said to my father later was this. That man next door says he owns all our houses. That man next door has a key to my house. That man next door watches me, and he comes in, I hear him. That's when she started, with those strong hands of hers, piling up the furniture, the chairs, the end tables I remember from the old house in Chicago, barricading herself against the threat of neighbors, against, perhaps, the advances of all the men she'd ever granted the attention of her batting eyelashes. Antony told me he'd come over and put the chairs and tables back in their places, and the next time he'd stop by her furniture was jumbled up against her front door again, while she sat in the TV room, staring in the direction of Fox News with the sound turned up so loud the man next door might have been able to hear.

Inset of Body Tectonics (Divergent)

Linnea says: Gram imagining the man next door has a key is like that jazz critic's description of Nancy Wilson's voice. When we fear something we don't hear what's really there, but rather what we imagine. Hasn't Gram always been worried that someone, one of those *other* kinds of people is chasing her?

I say: Gram hasn't said anything about what the man next door looks like.

Linnea says: Gram can't see, right? So who knows what she imagines she sees.

I say: That's true. She thinks of herself as having what those other people want. She still doesn't trust her daughter's husband, for instance, even though he's been her son-in-law for fifty years. She thinks she can still talk her daughter out of marrying that mill guy from the neighborhood. Those Italians, they're raised different, she says.

Linnea, always thinking of her East Coast Italian American mother, listens hard to what people say about Italians. Linnea says: Raised different sounds like *raced* different.

I say: Maybe. Remember after the O.J. Simpson trial, when it was on the news that O.J. was spending time on some golf course in Florida? Gram was sure she saw O.J. putting on the green behind her house.

Linnea says: Real things are replaced by what we fear. Some demented jazz critic in 1962 listens to Nancy Wilson's voice and hears she's as talented as anybody, maybe more talented, but still thinks he hears something savage.

I say: So then, if my grandmother knew anything about the real O.J., maybe she wouldn't have seen her imaginary O.J.?

Linnea says: Well, O.J.'s a difficult example.

I say: So is Nancy Wilson's dress. We think it's sexy too, right? We think that color suits her, makes her skin glow, right?

Linnea says: Her dress is sexy. It does make her skin glow.

Gram wouldn't like me to say she'd lost her eyelash-batting powers. She wanted more than anything to keep walking smoothly through rooms with her hair done and her head up. One Sunday, at a café near the beach, I saw her do just that. My dad had put together the event, a jazz brunch. He knew all the singers and musicians. He knew most of the people in the audience, and they all recognized Gram Rose. They all knew she couldn't see, could barely hear. But Rose knew the script. Jazz music is, to her, for dancing. Remember, she'd met her first husband, escaped her own immigrant family, while dancing to jazz. So even without being able to see where she was going she boogied between the tables and sidled up next to the trio. Her elbows flayed. Her head wagged. I understand now why they called it kicking up your heels, because I could see flashes of the soles of her shoes.

My dad is straddling a kitchen chair while Gram munches on her salad. The corner of her mouth is smudged with blue cheese. He's a great guy, she says, motioning to my dad. It's unclear whether she remembers, at this moment, who he is to her, but she does remember that he's the one who comes every day to make her this salad.

Naw, I was a bad kid, he repeats, half smiling. He's not a bad kid. Look what he's doing for his mother.

Oh you were never bad, she says.

What did you ever do that was so bad? I ask him.

Well, I smashed up my mother's car, he says. I hear him, but I don't think Gram does. She's wearing the cheap hearing aid, the one advertised on TV. My mother and father and Antony's wife have crawled under tables and pulled bedclothes from the bed, but they haven't been able to find the two good hearing aids from the doctor. The cheap one works sometime, if my mother holds it in her hand for a moment as if she were incubating an egg, and then shakes it until it lets out a high-pitched tone, a soprano moan we can hear across the kitchen, but the rest of the time it goes off and on, so we never know when Gram can really hear us. Plus Gram nods and laughs, engaged, cordial, as if she hears.

You smashed up Gram's car? I ask. This is a story I haven't heard before.

What? Gram asks, really listening again. It's probably the word *car* that got her attention. She misses hers. She misses driving to the store and the beauty parlor and church by herself. She would never say it, but I think she misses being free of her family.

I was taking your mother home from a date, driving her back to the Projects, Dad says. I skidded on ice and rammed a parked car.

An accident? That could have happened to anyone.

I wasn't supposed to have her car.

Ah. I nodded. So he'd had a date. He hadn't asked permission.

Gram hadn't approved of my mother, that girl in the Capri pants from the Projects. Still I doubt it was the unauthorized use of his mother's car he was thinking about, nearly fifty years later, but something else. Rebellion. Pulling away. He probably doesn't always want to make his mother dinner, night after night, not because he's bad, but because he's a normal, regular human, because it's tiring to be daily forgotten by your own mother, because he made himself into a man who loved things his mother was afraid of, such as jazz that is for listening instead of dancing, but none of that mattered between 5:30 and 5:45, because it was time to make his mother's dinner.

Whether or not Sundowner's Syndrome is the right way to describe it, I'm not too surprised that Gram thinks the guy next door is watching her. She's always feared that men were watching her. Everything she possesses—her home, her car, her glamour girl gait—is matched by her fears of what could be taken away. My brother Paulie has stories of fruitless all-night stakeouts on the roof of Gram's suburban Chicago ranch house when he was in high school, all because Gram was certain she saw some man peering in from the backyard window. Her imagination has always been peopled with Peeping Toms.

Gram, I say, why would the man next door watch you? Don't you think he's too busy? She will never say what I believe to be true. That her man next door is some part of herself she won't admit to, the gritty old East Side avenues, the gurgle in her dying husband's throat, the messy body itself, underneath the dance steps, the improvisational counterbeat none of us can control.

He wants my house, she tells me. He wants in. Do you know he has a key?

Inset of Navigating Jazz (Variation)

The thing about jazz is the downbeat, the turnabout, which requires migration from one kind of listening to another.

I don't listen to the same era of jazz as my father. Dad and Linnea prefer the same mid-1950s bebop and West Coast cool, their reversals held between notes of set expectation. They like to hear a theme, repeating, adhered to, even if in between those brackets the keyboard or horn riff or guitar strings go eccentric. They prefer improvisation with an anchor. Me, I prefer the broken-down walls of John Coltrane and Ornette Coleman, the patterning that comes of breath and prayer, intuition before formal commitment.

But across these variations the fact of the downbeat is the same. The thing about jazz musicians, the early ones who changed the way we listen, is they thrived as artists, black or white, on an arc of human improvisation, at a time in history, the American 1950s and '60s, when African Americans were still barred from full American citizenry. The downbeat was a discovery of human resistance, of human extrapolation, illuminating the humanness of the form's inventors, in spite of law or history or limits in the cartographic vision of the guys who sold the records. And the discovery of jazz by urban white ethnic guys like my father—though probably tainted, as we all are tainted, by advertising—was also a discovery of the possibilities for humans to expand, for maps to merge, for the banished body, any body, to remap against history.

I can't say exactly what my father and Linnea hear when they listen to their jazz, but for me it's a kind of traveling, an ongoing migration. The pierce of a horn, spiraling, rising, then interrupted by the bell notes and accumulated trills of the piano keys, carry my body from the stasis of the room to the longed-for and skittering horizon. I wonder if it was the same for my father, not transgression so much as the wonder of remaking, what any of us wants to learn about ourselves between the time we depart our family home and the time we find ourselves growing old in our own.

This could be the same reason our family took road trips—Dad driving us, when I was a girl, in his truck camper all the way through Canada, then down into Mexico. Part of the reason for those trips may have been simply the fact of 29.9 cents-per-gallon gas and my parents' public schoolteacher jobs that left those summers open, sure, but the real motivation was my father's wish to encounter an unfamiliar turn. How often did my two brothers, my mother, and I swelter in the back of the camper, parked at the side of the road, while my dad took his time lingering over another long camera shot, devoid of people, his attention focused on the curves and bellows of a landscape miles beyond the home he'd chosen, or that had chosen him. These summer-long road trips had been my father's idea, after all, his reprieve from his high school classroom, weeks of wandering south from Chicago, recording a map made of his undiluted stare.

In a photograph from one of those summers, I hold my father's map of Mexico, outstretched in front of my body, my long blond braids crowning the shot. My father's planned route is inked in black marker, down one side of the country to the tip of the Yucatán Peninsula and back up the other side into California. A casual observer might assume the photograph is a portrait of my father's daughter, but I am just the lovely assistant. The subject of the photograph is the jazz of Dad's wanderlust. What else might he find out there, turnabout from his mother's influence, on the land located downbeat from Chicago, in the bent note motoring from Cannon Adderley's horn?

Inset of the Downbeat

My dad used to argue with me when I was a teenager, trying to talk me into loving jazz. He'd hear my Joni Mitchell albums filtering through the walls of my bedroom and wait for me to come out, with his record player all cued up. If you like that stuff then you should listen to this, he told me, and he'd play tracks from the American Songbook, singers like Nancy Wilson. Listen to that tone, listen to that range, he'd say to me, and I'd sit there on my mother's blue brocade sofa staring out the front-room picture window as Miss Nancy sang "Lush Life" or "Midnight Sun." These are the great American songs, my dad told me. These are songs that will stop me in my tracks today, but back then I couldn't be bothered.

But did she *write* the song? I asked. No, he said. She's an interpreter. I rolled my eyes. The real creative ones, in my opinion—in all my 1970s teenage free-form-hippie wisdom—were the singer/ songwriters. If they didn't write their own songs it wasn't personal, it wasn't expression, I said.

I don't know if Dad had any better luck convincing my mother. Once Mom figured out I'd been reading her letters she hid them before I finished. I tried to find the letters again, and did once, a few years later, in another dresser shoved in the corner of the basement laundry room, but then she hid them once more and I haven't seen them since. So I never found out if Dad converted her. If I ask her she might say she loves jazz, of course she loves jazz, or she might say jazz is my father's thing, that she likes Broadway, but her response may have less to do with jazz than with moods in their marriage I am not equipped to read. So did Dad teach his wife to love jazz, or has she just become accustomed, as I have become accustomed to Linnea's football games and crime investigation TV shows, even watching with her from time to time, only because it's a way for us to be together?

I didn't begin to listen to jazz myself until around the time I fell in love with Linnea. It started with another album, music that was only sort of jazz but with a jazz babe on the album jacket. This was Julie London's *Julie Is My Name*, an album I'd stolen from my parents' house before I moved away for good. The photo background was pale green. Julie's hair was a blondish red. I remember her in a floor-length, glove-tight evening gown, but when I find a picture of the album I see that I just imagined the dress. The image cuts off at her cleavage, so she might be wearing a strapless gown, might be wearing a bustier, might be wearing nothing at all. If Nancy Wilson's record promoters were selling a yellow dress against caramel-colored skin, Julie London's promoters were selling the canyon cleavage of an icily assimilated white girl.

When I fell in love with Linnea and she loved jazz and got me to love it too—the same exact stuff my dad tried to get me to listen to when I was in high school—together we listened to my dad's old Julie

London album, agreed that the orchestration was too thick, agreed this was not even jazz, not really, but it was still something I liked, and something my dad liked once, enough to buy it. I don't know if the cover art had anything to do with it. Her sad stony face. Her tawny polished skin. Her hair swept off her forehead and tumbling down her back. Her bare breasts that seemed to tremble in the soft green light. This was a smoky nightclub, dry martini, leave your mother's home sort of album.

That my father had this album told me that once he'd wanted to leave home, as I did when I left and took this album with me. That's part of what he meant, I think, when he told his old mother he was a bad son. I watch my father feed his mother her dinner as if she is his child, and I notice the smear of dressing on the corner of Gram's mouth, my dad's resigned smile as he watches, knowing she can't see whether he's there or not. I only come around to watch once a year. So who's the bad kid?

Gram is shaking a clothes hanger at us. The shirt on the hanger is a shimmered synthetic with a matching belt. If Gram wasn't standing there holding it I would have thought: That looks like the kind of shirt Gram would wear, the kind of shirt that she bought because it looked classy to her.

Someone is leaving their clothes in my closet, she tells us, shaking the hanger again. She is standing in front of a photograph of herself as she talks, one of hundreds that hang on her walls. Everyone in the family is up on that wall somewhere, along with a shot of a 1970s beach blonde with tan lines, smiling over her shoulder at the camera, her buttocks and nipples bare, a snapshot Antony slipped into the corner of a frame twenty years or so ago, as a joke, and never took down again. Gram was always a good one for going along with jokes, especially if they were that bat-your-eyelashes-at-men sort of naughty.

The shot she's standing in front of is a photo of herself at a banquet, from back in the day when she still had functions in her life, a fancy dinner where she is wearing the same shirt she's shaking at us now. I've never seen this shirt before, she says. But Gram, that's your shirt, I say. I've seen you wear that shirt. No no, my clothes are nice. I only have good clothes. Those people next door come in here and leave their clothes. Why would they do that? I ask her. They are trying to take over, she says.

I think she must mean that she's feeling herself slipping away. Not her body itself but the image of her body, the space around her body. There's nothing left to keep alight her album jacket version of herself, the American nurse in the alabaster city, wearing white hose and a starched white dress, hair pinned and poofed, making her forehead appear stronger, her expression no-nonsense, composed, a professional face, the first you meet when approaching the receptionist's window in the Michigan Avenue doctor's waiting room, a face that dispenses, nods, and agrees to open doors. You couldn't see the old East Side on the image she'd made of her body, not the streetcars or the docks or the train tracks or the smell of grainy Old World coffee and heavy breads baking in the oven and men who get kicked around by the company and then go home and kick around the women. She is losing the map of the body she had longed for, exposing the map beneath, a topography of the mortal body itself.

They don't make LPs anymore, only CDs and digital downloads, so the cover art is smaller. When the borders lose their constancy, when the neighbors start invading, when you get so old and skinny your clothes don't fit you, when you become certain your clothes belong to someone else, what's left? A lemon yellow dress. A stretch of music that bends unexpectedly. A borrowed car skidding on the ice. A bad daughter who leaves her family and doesn't tell them where she's going. A bad son who doesn't really leave, but imagines life might have been different if he had. The past banging on the window to get in but posing as the man next door. Twirling at a park district dance with the man you'll marry. A son who comes over, or is it a grandson? He makes a darn good salad. Fragments of ground we left home to find. Fragments of ground we once, so badly, needed to leave.

Inset of Legend and Contour (Alternate View)

Linnea and I saw Miss Nancy Wilson perform at the Blue Note in Manhattan. The room was crowded, two or three couples per table. Was the interior light actually blue, or am I just remembering it that way? We sat, in a packed house of more black people than white, with a nice middle-aged African American straight couple. We never asked if they were from out of town too. I don't recall what I was wearing but probably the usual V-neck, cleavage-baring dress, maybe the one with a black-and-white lace pattern; yellow is not my color. Linnea was probably wearing her fedora with the feather in the brim, but she would have certainly taken off the hat before the show started and set it on the table between us. The man kept looking at Linnea. We'd seen this before, that look of trying to figure out the foreigner, and we were sure he had the usual question. Is that one a man or a woman?

Nancy was of course no longer the sassy gal in the yellow dress. Her hair, laced with gray, was swept up in a neat French twist, the kind Gram Rose used to wear. Her jacket was embroidered with sequins that caught the stage lights. But her voice was the same. When she sang about the midnight sun Linnea sidled up next to me and slipped a hand under my thigh, reminding me again that the whole point of longing is to finally obtain.

Between sets I went out to use the restroom and look over the items in the gift shop. I wanted something for Dad. A baseball hat with "Blue Note Jazz" embroidered across the front. A golf shirt with the logo on the pocket. Even after all his years devoted to jazz, Dad had never been to a New York jazz club. While I leaned over the glass display case a waiter walked behind me with a tray of food and knocked on the door to my right. The dressing room popped open and there she was, Fancy Miss Nancy, this time in her robe and stocking feet. I noticed her feet in particular, her hose a little twisted, so that her big toe looked to be out of joint. Nancy Wilson's toe, I thought, and then looked up at her face, accidentally catching her eye.

Our glances met for just a moment. I can't claim that anything in particular passed between us. I didn't tell her that jazz remade my dad and that my dad made me. I didn't tell her about how he'd tried to get me to listen to her music as a girl, and that I'd refused him. I didn't even tell her how many times I'd listened to her version of "Guess Who I Saw Today" and how each time I imagined I was there with her, wearing a sweet wool shopping-in-Manhattan suit with a knee-length skirt and big buttoned jacket, sitting alone at a white-covered table, and each time I cried with her. I didn't ask if Linnea and I were welcome in the country she sang us through, and that perhaps my father heard as well, the country pictured on the jackets of her old albums. I didn't say I wished my dad had come with us to hear her too. I didn't mention that I knew the woman on her album jacket was a map of other people's dreams, not an actual woman, and that hearing her live was more than listening to her record. I didn't even ask if she still had that yellow dress.

All I did was look at her, eye to eye. Perhaps she longed to hear some gush of love from a jazz fan. Perhaps I longed for the longing of my youth. We looked at each other for a second, with curiosity, that's all, across, or within, a country or two.

FIG. 15. *Islandia* by Abraham Ortelius, 1587.

FIG. 15. *Islandia* by Abraham Ortelius, 1587.

Some cartographers choose to illuminate the monsters.

MAP 7

Here Be Monsters

A cartography of the prairie, with
overlays and panorama feature

Urbana, Illinois, is not a town I would choose to return to. Not that
there's anything wrong with Urbana itself, one of the Tree City USA
communities where the trees still form a densely woven canopy and
some of the winding streets are still paved with brick. The main campus
of the University of Illinois sits at the center of things, straddling the
boundary between the twin towns of Champaign and Urbana, and the
wide cornfields that have supplanted the old midwestern prairie circle
the populated grid. The land itself is flatter than flat, the expanse so
wide and open that gazing out on the horizon feels a bit like staring out
at an uncharted sea, and that hard prairie wind has little to obstruct it
here, a constant pitch hard enough to straighten curly hair and wear
flags down to a nub.

When I was a skinny blond undergraduate in this prairie college
town I wore short denim skirts and lacy camisole leotards without a
bra. Straight guys I knew then recalled me later as a long-legged girl
with a hard impenetrable expression and blond pre-Raphaelite hair,
and I remember myself that way as well. But I know too that the curly
hair I wore then was a fiction, a perm. The truths and untruths of the
rest of my time in Urbana are harder to make out.

In the thirty years since then I've gone back only a few times, to see my middle brother, whose house rests on the far southern edge of town. My brother is a tall guy who never sits still. He mutters and putters, turns up the ballgame, gets upset when the Cubs or the Illini lose. Like me, Benny attended college in Urbana, but unlike me he stuck around to graduate. He eventually married a local girl and they have a son, so he'll probably never move back to our old home, Chicago.

Looking south from Benny's kitchen window all I can see is flat former farmland, a development purgatory, empty space, untilled and probably as close to the original prairie as it's been for a hundred years. Here be monsters, I want to say, but don't. Instead I tell Benny he should take a series of photos, shifting his body slightly to the right with each shot, so he can get at this whole wide horizon. This is the old prairie, a historic landscape, I tell him. You could mount the photos side by side, like the collage prints hanging in museums. I believe what I'm saying, but am also trying to convince myself to believe in the benign beauty of all this open space. Yes, photograph this before it's gone, I say.

I don't need to do that, Benny says. I can just use the panorama setting on my camera.

No, no I say. I shake my head. Not wide enough.

Overlay of Open Space

Old maps don't leave blank the open expanse of unexplored seas. On sixteenth-century maps of the island of Iceland, for instance, uncharted waters are crowded with menacing creatures. Sea horses with serpent's tails. Fish the size of ships with barbed noses and sharp-toothed grins. *Here Be Monsters* is the phrase attributed to medieval cartographers, used to mark the regions too dangerous or distant, as yet, to explore. The mapmakers' monsters circle their shorelines, menacing yet playful. The artists' renderings of what can't be charted are images of dread and pleasure both.

My spotty stories from the time I spent in Urbana are not exceptional. Nearly everyone I knew in the late 1970s drank too much and smoked too much dope. And who doesn't carry blank spots, unidentifiable open fields, uncharted expanses populated with private monsters?

The first time I tried to shake off Urbana was when I was in my midthirties, living in Minneapolis, a few years sober. I'd lived more than ten years as a lesbian by then, had finally finished college, had set up house with Linnea. By all accounts I was fine, and yet I knew something was wrong. My clothes, even the soft ones, even the pajamas all felt too scratchy, and I was all of a sudden dreaming, all the time, about drinking.

So I sought therapy. The first counselor I found with open appointments and a sliding fee scale turned out to be an art therapist. Her desk was covered in little clay figurines made by her clients, tiny bodies wearing red dresses, baggy pants, and jaunty hats. I wondered at first if the rest of her clients where children. The first exercise she asked me to try was to scribble abstract maps in a blank sketchbook, then talk about what I saw hidden in the crayon scrawl, a sort of Where's Waldo? of my unconscious. She wanted me to play with crayons? Her assignment seemed silly, but I gave it a try.

What I found in my automatic maps, or thought I found, or chose to find, was the same image over and over. Long or short. Straight or curved. I hadn't seen an actual penis in over a decade. Why would a lesbian find the landscape of her unconscious littered with penises? I was unnerved, yet couldn't stop, drawing after drawing more or less the same.

The drawings were random scrawls, the exercise designed, I presume, to lead me to construct interpretation, to trick myself, at age thirty-four, into becoming conscious of unexamined history, my life as it happened at age nineteen, the drinking, the blackouts, the vast terra incognita of uncharted memory, or worse, absence of memory, by which I mean less what was on my map than what I believed might be there.

Overlay of Open Space

When Linnea and I were tourists in Iceland in the late 1990s we saw an exhibit of Olafur Eliasson's landscape photography. On one side of the gallery the artist hung close-ups of Reykjavik houses, the same sort we'd walked past on the street outside. These were like no homes we'd ever seen before, double- or triple-storied, workmen's row houses with exteriors encased in corrugated aluminum and painted various colors of sherbet, with big windows and skylights, light catchers for the days that part of the world has only an hour or two of daylight. Icelandic city houses are utilitarian yet festive, and the photographs of these houses were mounted in square frames and hung close to one another, hunched together as if shoulder-to-shoulder, congested like a city neighborhood.

The opposite wall of the gallery held contrary horizons, broad instead of clustered. Wide lava fields and misty geothermal lagoons were printed in panorama format, prairies of cold lava and blue steam. The effect was widening, as if the community breath held on one side of the room was exhaled on the other. Linnea and I stood in the center, looking at one side, then turning to look again at the other, our shoulders touching. The houses were reflected in the glass of the landscapes, and the landscapes in the glass of the houses, the gallery a mirrored interior of Iceland, its regions calling over and across to each other, the country's entire geography imaged at once, breadth and depth.

It's not the prairie's fault. That it is wide and flat is one thing; that standing in the wind rocks me nearly off my feet is another. But open spaces don't create what people do within them, or to them, right?

Still, a blander landscape might be less potent all these years later, or even a landscape that had more going on. But every place, even open space, has a lot going on. I have a bad habit of mistaking architecture for life.

Geographically central Illinois is a happening place. Glacier geologists call what used to be here, during the Ice Age, the Wisconsin Drift, a country-size shovel of ice that tore up the earth, leaving a clean bowl a thousand miles wide, a space for bluestem, blazing star, and goldenrod, a place where the grass grew as tall as the two-story houses built on the prairie today. The first immigrants who saw this land, as it used to be, experienced a dry squall billowing and receding in the wind, no solid ground in sight.

Once upon a time there was the tall grass and then the corn and now finally all these years later the new homes, like my brother's, with basements and fenced yards and problems with field mice. If memory overlays and underlays the present, things that once happened here might reside in the tall weeds at the side of the road, or they might be mixed up, like dust and pollen, in wind itself. Or maybe not.

Panorama View, with Crossroads

Here was the time when I drove through that Illinois corn prairie. I was with my friend Verna, right after I'd dropped out of college, on our way up north to Chicago to catch a train.

I say Verna was my friend, but in truth I wanted her to be much more. I wanted to kiss her, and the night before our drive, when she stayed over at my apartment, with me in my bed, I let my calves and wrists bump up against her back, pretending it was an accident, hoping she would get the hint, and oh god of course she did, but she must not have wanted to because she didn't turn around, didn't kiss me on the mouth and stroke my hair the way I hoped she would. I was too scared then to ask her straight out, even though I had been with women by then, even if not yet with a woman I loved. Then again, it could also be my desires weren't as obvious to Verna as I thought.

Verna lived out in the corn, in an old farmhouse. Near harvest time the corn grew tall on all sides, as tall as the old tallgrass, taller than any of our heads, swaying and righting itself again, delicate bodies, a green ballet. Verna lived cheaply. We all did then. I lived in a studio in town, with a closet-size kitchen and an alcove for my bed, an old mattress on the floor. The house I live in now in Minneapolis, with Linnea, a modest 1904 two-story Queen Anne cottage, full of furniture and televisions and appliances, is ostentatious when I compare.

Verna wore her thin, husk-colored hair cut short across her forehead, cute bangs, and she always wore mismatched socks. Her words were spare and specific, but her voice was airy, full of space and wind. Thinking of her now I can see why she might have seemed to me then some kind of antidote to my monsters—all that clean wind and space in her—but that's too simple an interpretation. Pining for my girlfriends was nothing new. For as long as I could remember I'd been falling in love with women from afar, the only difference now being that I recognized the feeling for what it was.

And what druggy 1970s romantic wouldn't fall for Verna, living as she did in a plain white room with billowing white curtains and a white iron bed and scarves tied around the lampshades, like the set for one of those foggy hair band rock videos, though this was before MTV. Books, papers, record albums, bits of costume jewelry were piled on the floor. The first time I was there she showed me a pair of boots, ankle high with wicked heels. She said she stole them from her first woman lover, and she laughed. That was typical. She'd tell a story about herself, always a little outside the lines, and she'd laugh. I don't know if I laughed back. I remember myself then as always missing words, unable to speak, caught in the space of my still mostly unspeakable feelings.

This story is not only what it seems, a long slow drive through the prairie, a wide windy vista, with a woman I was smitten with but afraid to touch. At the time of year we traveled, just before spring planting, the dirt blew off the fields and across our windshield, sheets of brown dust sometimes thick enough to seem a dry rain. The drama of the dust and wind suited my mood, which was a sort of blue-gray happiness, because Verna wanted to spend this time with me.

But it was not so much friendship as happenstance that brought us into each other's company. What Verna and I really had in common then was we both were living halfway between the worlds of women-who-loved-women and women-who-loved-men. Our boyfriends, Leonard and CJ, had left Illinois and moved to Minnesota together. We were on our way to go see them, first by truck, then by train, sneaking away, making sure none of our lesbian friends heard what we were up to.

Some of the women that knew us both quizzed me later, trying to figure out if I was sleeping with Verna, but I never spilled.

So yes, it's true that Verna and I were traveling companions, but we were moving in opposite directions. Leonard was the last man I would be with before migrating all the way to women. CJ was Verna's first boyfriend, after a long string of women, on her path back to men. Leonard and CJ were best friends, bearded guys with batik shirts and ponytails, roommates, even occasional lovers, or so they said. I never actually saw that part. They were political men, radical men, their sexuality part of their political ground, and they described themselves to Verna and to me as bisexual.

We were all aware of the tensions. It was the late 1970s, the early identity years, when we were all supposed to pick one side of the street and stick to it. I didn't tell any of my new lesbian friends that I had a boyfriend. Verna met CJ when he was fixing the shingles on the house where she was still living with her lesbian lover, in a campus collective everyone who was even a little bit alternative knew about, because it was the place where all the lesbians lived.

Before I'd even met Verna I'd heard the story of her falling in love with the man who was working on the roof of her house, where she lived with the best-known lesbian activist in town, a woman with broad shoulders and red hair and a temper big as the prairie. I should have wondered then over this narrative, told to me by Leonard, who heard it from the roof man, CJ—a story about lesbians as narrated by men. I don't mean to suggest these were dishonorable men, but in their view of the world lesbians were women-who-loved-women who also slept with *them*, and to be fair, that's just who these two guys were sleeping with then—one former lesbian, one future.

Verna's angry lover was a woman with a sharp mind and hard wit who'd later be a good friend of mine, and she was no more or less flawed than the rest of us then, but the guys described her to me as a mythical figure—Anger is Woman—pelting CJ with loose shingles and shouting him off the roof. To be fair the dude had stolen her girlfriend, and who among us hasn't at some point in our lives lost our shit when a lover jilts us, but back then we said we didn't believe in monogamy or possessiveness.

What Verna believed in then I'm not entirely sure, but soon after she moved out into the corn.

Overlay of the Needle

Years after I'd rehashed what went wrong for me on the Illinois prairie, I started to notice that recovery stories had become a staple of popular culture. The TV stations that had once played only music were now running talking-head documentaries about the same musicians who would otherwise have appeared in rock videos. These programs weren't called drunk-a-logues or drug-a-logues, but that's what they were. All these stories had the same pattern, a strictly linear story structure borrowed directly from AA. *What it was like. What happened. What it's like now.*

In one episode of this program members of a rock band whose crash-and-burn style of music is not anything I would ever listen to, but whose drug-a-logue had me riveted, talked about bottoming out on heroin. I *woke up*, said the bass guitarist, and the needle was *still* in my *arm, man.* He said it with a smirk that tells us he knows it's not funny exactly, and yet it's funny as hell, because he should have died but didn't. What happened? He cheated the Reaper, and now he was telling his story on TV.

I don't repeat his story now because my own sobering up was anything like what happened to this fellow. Rather I'm thinking about a mythic character, the rock star, his bottle-black hair, his tattooed stomach and pierced eyebrow and all of the other parts of his body collapsed on some floor somewhere, getting ready to die. But then he doesn't die. His phoenix rises. He finds not Jesus, but something like Jesus, and he is restored, and now his whole life turns on this memory of that moment when everything changed. Or so he says. He doesn't say whether he ever dreams of that needle, whether there are places he visits that whisper to him, *Take the needle, beautiful needle,* whether there are mornings he wakes up and wonders if the needle is still in his arm.

Panorama View, with Crossroads

I met Leonard at one of my part-time jobs in a campus bar. Although he was a doctoral student then he looked the counterculture-carpenter type with his worn work boots and canvas utility vest with tool loops, nothing like the skinny boys with sensitive typewriter fingers and perpetually stoned smiles in my writing classes or who worked with me on the college newspaper staff. Right away, after spending a few nights with him, I found out Leonard had another lover, a bisexual British woman in town temporarily to work for the National Women's Music Festival, a big lesbian event crowding the campus for a week every June that intrigued me but that I was still too scared to attend.

I met the Bisexual Brit briefly, remember her knees exposed just under the hem of her baggy hemp-colored dress, her flat sandals, and the way we stared at each other across Leonard's porch and then both silently nodded. It was painful, this idea of sharing a lover, but then again this was all part of it, my choosing of Leonard, a new bisexual territory without recognizable rules, a route toward my still-to-materialize new world appearing like a tunnel opening in the prairie grass. Previously implausible liaisons now seemed possible.

There were other men whose touch I responded to more heatedly than I did Leonard's, although not so much if I compare to the way I thought about Verna without the benefit of touching—her face, her eyes, the airy lilt of her voice, and those ridiculous socks. Do straight women feel that way about the men they desire, that feeling of wanting to put your lips everywhere, that wish to climb between their fleshy thighs and sweat? Gay men have told me they do, and their stories are my best point of reference. Leonard was my good friend, a sensitive bed partner, a nice man nearly fifteen years older than I whom I hurt when I finally left, even though he had to have seen it coming. When I said I loved him I meant I was devoted. Not on fire.

Somewhere in my boxes and albums of snapshots I have a photograph of the four of us then: bushy-bearded Leonard in a flannel workshirt, CJ with his long black hair and well-tended yogi beard,

Verna with her hair cut in those cute bangs, wearing the rust-red corduroy pants I loved, and me in flannel plaid as well, as I'd stopped wearing anything girlish, my still partly permed hair pulled messily back from my face. The photo was taken during Verna's and my trip to Minnesota, in Leonard's utilitarian south Minneapolis apartment, the upper duplex of a house that's since been torn down, where we sat on square wooden furniture he'd built himself. The way I remember the photograph we are arranged foursquare, the camera set on a table, the shutter tripped by a timer. The four of us formed a literal crossroads, and it wouldn't be long before we'd all scatter in four directions.

Where did we go from there? If I had snapshots of the sequel, if I could thumb through them fast, as if viewing a movie flip book, I'd watch me, migrating up to Minneapolis for good and living two doors down from Leonard, but never with him, and CJ moving back to some comfortable suburb of Chicago, cutting off all that fine black hair, answering the phone curtly when Verna calls him, years later, acting as if he is ashamed of her, or himself, and telling her to leave him alone. I'd watch Verna fall in love with a Wisconsin man who lives in a perpetually half-built house in a Lake Michigan resort town, and then give birth to a daughter she names after a bird. I'd watch Leonard hanging out at the 400 Bar in the old hippie district of Minneapolis—by that time I am his only lover—while I sleep with one woman and then another until I finally fall in love with a visiting lesbian playwright on a Sunday morning, on a messy futon on the floor of another crumbling upper duplex, my old Pinto parked conspicuously in front. In this last shot my phone is ringing and ringing and ringing and I'm not picking up because I know it's Leonard, who only has to look out his front window to see I'm home, ignoring his calls.

But before, in the first photograph, none of this has happened yet. The way I recall the picture Verna and I sit next to each other, the guys behind us. Leonard looks at me sweetly. Verna and CJ look into each other's eyes. I gaze at Verna, remembering what she said to me on the drive up from central Illinois on our way to ride Amtrak's *Empire Builder* from Chicago to Minneapolis, the dry April dust billowing around her truck like miniature twisters. The prairie, she said, the prairie is blowing away, and I could see she meant literally, yes. But even then I knew more than just the topography was changing.

Overlay of Open Space

When Linnea and I were on that Iceland trip we took a ride through the lava fields in one of the minivans that carted tourists all over the island. We were on our way back to our Reykjavik hotel from the Blue Lagoon, a bright blue geothermal pool with lathery sheets of steam rising from the water, thick enough to make us feel we'd been swimming through a Cirque de Soleil set.

The Blue Lagoon is located miles outside of the city and is surrounded on all sides by a prairie of hardened lava. The ground in all directions is rocky and bumpy, the texture gnarled, like charcoal burned into the bottom of a grill—a grill the size of an island. Even the ancient maps display this quality, the coast of the island as coarse and uneven as those lava fields, a surface so eerie it's not hard to believe the surrounding waters could be, as the ancient cartographers feared, crowded with mutant creatures born of all that thermal pressure. A green moss grows over and around the lava, so the panorama view is both soft and jagged. If indeed here be monsters, a woman might escape over that landscape, but she'd never get away without tripping and scraping her elbows and knees.

The tour van was full of military men; Linnea and I guessed they were servicemen on weekend furlough from the U.S. Air Force base in Greenland. They were burly guys with stubble cut hair and booming voices, complaining about their hangovers and talking about women and queers in ways that made Linnea's and my backs stiffen. Linnea muttered, Here we go, and I turned to her and she turned to me, and when our eyes met I knew she and I were thinking the same thing. *Get us out of this van.*

We saw nothing but lava and moss and wisps of steam for miles. We've traveled to many cities together—New York, Rome, Tokyo, Amsterdam—and have occasionally been stared down by angry-looking men who called us freaks or unnatural women, but cities seem to be, if not my alabaster dream space, then at least some kind of haven, with plenty of people to hear us yell for help. This mottled Icelandic plain, so barren and rough-hewn—where would we go if we tried to run away?

Panorama View, with Crossroads

I talk about my own open spaces as if I believe our lives are mappable. Yet when I finally dug out the evidence of that old crossroads photograph of Leonard and me, Verna and CJ, I was almost sorry I'd looked, because I found I'd remembered completely wrong; this was not, after all, the memory that would finally map me. In the actual photo we four are lined up in a row, arranged by couples. Leonard and I are side by side, Verna and I are in the middle, CJ is on Verna's other side. The picture portrays two apparently heterosexual couples, sidling close. Everyone looks straight into the camera, except me. I look at Leonard, sweetly.

Did Leonard mean more to me than I remember? Did I need to forget my feelings for him in order to finally fall in with a woman? Was he my lover or my protector? Were we all not at the crossroads? This is supposed to be that mythic bird's part of the awakening, where the heroine comes to herself, makes this last stop with a bisexual man who tells her stories about her new lesbian friends, and once she finds them she is better, newly and accurately mapped, at last.

But this assumes that once we slay monsters, here be no more monsters. Missing here is another map, the one on which we learn to live without the projection of some mythically pristine city where all our familiar monsters have fled.

Underlay Where Be My Monsters

I recall the place, those Illinois fields, more than my body, or his body. The house belonged to a professor at this university where I was just a sophomore, before I knew Leonard, or Verna, a man who lived alone so far out into the corn that I wouldn't have been able to find my way home had I been lucid enough to try.

It's not that he threatened; it's just that he was a teacher, someone whose job it was to be attuned to the fragilities of the young, and probably too I loved, at first, being singled out by an older man in a campus-town night of a thousand drunk girls, but I was just so drunk, too drunk, by the time I was in his car, squinting in and out of blackout.

There was only one of him so it wasn't a gang-bang, but every time I see one of those scenes in a movie—the boys lined up, the girl in the back of a car—I've thought, Oh right, that's how it felt, the punishing fuck, the over and over, this speechless drunk girl, her unconsciousness perhaps the mainstay of her appeal. Until I was not so drunk anymore, the prairie outside brightening with thin yellow light before he finally stopped.

Decades later I looked at faculty photos on the university website to see if I'd recognize the corn man, a professor of science or engineering, or at least that's what he told the obviously intoxicated undergraduate girl he met in a bar. But I couldn't remember the fine points of his appearance. Wasn't his mud-colored hair long enough to curl behind his ears? Weren't his lips thin and tight? Scrolling through the faculty pages I realized, as far as I knew, Corn Man might be any one, or none, of those aging professors.

Terms like *date rape* and *consensual sex*—whatever they might mean to a girl spotting in and out of a booze blackout—weren't part of the parlance of 1978, and I'd been one of so many drunk girls in the Illinois campus bars when the drinking age was still just nineteen. Corn Man must not have been the only man in town aware that such happenings among the female undergrads were as common as corn. When what happens to a young woman has no clear name it follows that the experience has, for her, no discernible meaning—at least that's how it was for me before I understood what it meant to consent.

But what bothers me still is less the memory than the story I told myself after. That I was out there in the corn because I meant to be. That I was conscious, that if he'd asked me a question I could understand his meaning, that I'd had the wits to decide, yes, I want this; I will participate. That my fundamental landscape—my body and the body of the prairie, the body of my whole midwestern home, made of all I would do and have done to me in this formative time and space, the map I'd make all my later maps against—could be for me, or for anyone, a utopian construction of chosen elements, like a city planner's chart of the perfect city, all rounded edges and proportionate balance, free of any overgrown patches that thirty years later would be impossible to fully survey.

A few weeks afterward, at one of my jobs, cleaning the upper deck tables of a campus music club at the end of the night, which was really morning, the bars open until 2 a.m. in Illinois then, I saw Corn Man again. His was not the first insult of the evening. First another guy I knew from one of my classes found me up there a half hour before closing with a dirty rag in my hand and said, You work here? My classmate was a rumpled, solid fellow, not one of the sensitive artistic boys but rather the type of guy who'd looked like somebody's husband since he was twelve; he must have been a rich kid from one of the wealthy suburbs of Chicago, because why else would he be so bothered that his classmate was working in a bar? He asked, You work so late? The look on his face revealed his meaning—*So I knew you were on your way down, and now here you are, and I wish I could save you but I can't*—and then he handed me a $5 bill, an enormous tip for a cocktail waitress in a 1979 campus-town club who hadn't even served him a drink.

And then my classmate was gone and Corn Man appeared, thinner than I remembered him, standing next to me as I stacked chairs, stroking his five o'clock shadow like a chess player. I stacked one chair onto the other, and as they slipped into place Corn Man crooned, Nice fit, and he grinned at me as my stomach turned over. Ha-ha, I said and went back to work, keeping my back turned to him until he left.

A few weeks later, sitting in my dorm apartment, in a chair facing the picture window, I was unable to change out of my robe, unable to open a book or even move, and even then I thought this was only because of that tumbling prairie sky, because it was an impossibly cloudy day.

Underlay of a Body Politic

What then is the relationship of the lesbian to the penis? Some would say there is no relationship; some would say it depends; some would say that even asking the question is a misunderstanding of lesbian sexuality, of the intricacies of meaningful pleasures, of what makes a woman, what makes a man, of the nature of desire, of consensual, conscious fucking, of the barriers any of us may wish to break with a lover when we are sentient enough to choose the breaker, the breaking.

And so what then of my poppy fields of crayoned penises? In these past thirty years the categories of so many bodies—queer-identified bodies in particular—have changed. Any particular penis might be, from a biological woman's point of view, beside the point, too much focused on the peculiarities of bodies, too little on a body politic. My own sexual preference for women over men more and more seems to me a social rather than a biological pull, which might make me foundationally bisexual, or fluid, or simply incapable of seeing most people anymore as merely male, merely female. These days I interpret the phallic garden that emerged in my therapy scribbling as more map than territory, referring less to one trauma than to a time, an ethos, a point of captivity.

Overlay of Open Space

Maps are made of more than facts, are histories of what we believed, loved, feared, as well as who we actually were. Those monsters on the old maps, emerging from the northern brine, circling Iceland with teeth glittering in the midnight sun, where someone, a mapmaker, centuries ago, imagined they swam, suggest the ways wonder and injury might inhabit the same seas.

Bird's-Eye View of the Lesbian City

But what is the route from there to here? Years after I finished art therapy there was a night when this happens. Three lesbians go to a downtown Minneapolis sex toy store. This is Sex in the Lesbian City. Pale blue and purple light from the neon sign outside flickers across their faces. The three women are friends, never lovers, yet what they have in common are less the women they are than the women they love. All three are women who might pass as straight, except when accompanied by lovers butch enough to be, at times, the sort of women that strangers mistake for men, at which point the three lesbian friends are likely mistaken for straight again.

Two of these three lesbian friends mean to buy the third a dildo, for her birthday. Whatever you want, they tell her. They pick up tacky items like edible panties, like blow-up boobs, and they laugh, say Eeuh and Ick, and put them down again. This is not one of the clean feminist toy stores that will be easy to find in the city a few years later, the kind with pillows and curtains and tea. The place these three lesbians go shopping—Sex World, it's called—is a garish casino-like joint located on a quiet intersection in a noirish corner of the city.

There are several kinds of dildos available. Some are long sleek rockets with a vibrator inside, available in purple, pink, and leopard print. Some are a silicone, made to feel like flesh but the color of a tie-dyed shirt, their shape neutral, a cylinder with an indeterminate purpose. Some are anatomically correct, in various sizes and flesh tones, meant to be used with a harness. One of the women—okay this one is me—picks up one of the rockets. This is a good one to start with, she says. It doesn't look at all like a cock. Her friend picks up the other kind. It bobs and sways in her hand. This is the only kind I'd buy, she says. It's supposed to look like a cock, she says, and then she whispers, *That's the whole point.* The birthday girl shakes her head. Yuk, she says. Yuk. I don't like any of them. Let's get out of here.

So we didn't buy our friend a dildo, but my friend's comment lingered. What did lesbians like my friends and me—the ones who fall in love with women who live at the crossroads of male and female—think we were doing with dildos shaped like wavy lines or rocket ships? They are tools well made for the job they perform, but lack something of the slip-slide linguistics of sex and gender, are missing the reverb of signification. Why attempt to hide the past when the deepest stimulation requires the vibe of the underlay?

And what game do we, women like me, who long for the kisses of gentlemanly women, think we're playing? Toys are fun because they are toys. So then which games are the sex toy stores selling us, if not a *What if*? As in, What if fun-with-a-phallus does not belong strictly to the biologically male-female fuck? As in, What if you are the one with a cock and I am the one who will say yes, if the cock is the kind that rises to my benefit?

Underlay of a Girl, with Panorama View

While I am searching for that picture of Verna and me, Leonard and CJ, I find another that I didn't know I had, from before I knew any of them. It's a photo booth shot of Pre-Raphaelite Girl, the young woman who Corn Man took out into the prairie. Her inaccessible face. Her messy corkscrew hair the color of dried cornstalks. I go to the Internet and search with the words *Pre-Raphaelite Hair* and I find sites about paintings and phrases like *innocent attraction* and *enigmatic feminine* and *carnal loveliness*. I find a discussion question for a college course: *Why are these women attractive? Are they powerful? Or being possessed and caught within the frame?*

I see a young woman possessed by the frame of one story and then another. I see a woman who drank to make herself smaller even as she told herself she meant to get larger. I see her as if she were one of the students in my class the semester I taught writing at a tiny college forty-five minutes outside of Minneapolis, at a school I could get to quickest by driving south from my house, across the suburbs first, then looping through open Minnesota farmland that reminds me a little bit of the Illinois prairie—land that is much more hilly but just as exposed.

If the girl in that old picture came to my office with those evasive eyes, with another unbelievable reason why she didn't turn in her paper, I'd want to slap her face and shake those sloping shoulders. I'd want to beg her to run away through a tunnel in the grass.

When I widen the frame I see better the young woman I was, the summer after Corn Man, a little red baseball bat stuck out of her backpack as she trudged across the windy spaces of the university, because she had come to expect some unnamable trouble. She forgot this particular caution a few years later, when she might have needed it more, walking alone through Minneapolis at night, but then, in Urbana, age twenty, she actually practiced whipping the bat out and holding it over her head like a fearsome cartoon warrior. I see her too, turning away from guys who had been her friends, the ones who used to stay up all night with her, giggling, pointing at the people they found extreme or outlandish—people like the person she was about to become.

Since then, sometimes, but less often than before, if the vibe is strained or the space too open, I've had to work to make conversation with men who remind me even remotely of the men I knew in Urbana, unless they're gay or one of my brothers. There are still times, rare now, when I want to run away from a regular conversation because I hear the whisper—*beautiful needle*—and feel myself fall into that unconscious girl I used to be.

But that's not the prairie's fault. Standing on my brother's back deck, at the edge of this cornfield that once was tallgrass, or driving with my car windows down, past the stand of spiraling windmills just before the Wisconsin border, on my way home, I'm willing to let that hard wind straighten my hair, willing to line up snapshot after snapshot until I see the Illinois prairie as a breathless flat expanse where more than one kind of plant is able to grow.

Sometimes a prairie is just a prairie, and sometimes it's more. The part of that girl who remains is the same girl, now, who runs her hand through the field of Linnea's short, sharp hair and asks her to bring out the feels-like-real toy, a girl who's come to want little else from love than a lover willing to fuck her past her monsters.

FIG. 16. *Mississippi River Meander Belt* by Harold Fisk, 1944.

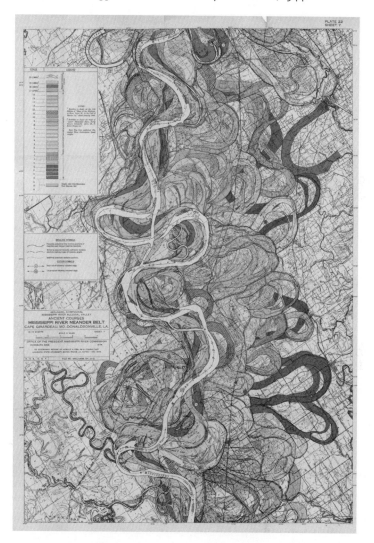

For don't we all live on waterfront property?

Waterfront Property
New Orleans itinerary, with
overlooks and meanderings

Water pulls the body forward. Water hems the body in. Nothing feeds longing like uncertainty, and nothing is more uncertain than a horizon line where the wide haze of water swallows the hard border of sky.

TripTik New Orleans: Look, I shouted to my father. I was the one who spotted her. My role, as my father's inquisitive daughter, is to be the one who points things out. She was the alabaster lady of the New World, the statue inviting wanderers to her shore, standing there at the gateway like a imperious guardian angel, like the rich lady who owned the joint.

The monument to the immigrants, on the New Orleans waterfront where the Mississippi rolls past the French Quarter, was another version of Columbia Gem of the Ocean, hers an amalgam of American body beautifuls—breasts and belly sheathed in white drapery, toes grazing the river, long hair blowing back toward the land, right hand raised to the portside sky the way a TV evangelist choir mistress holds the palms of her hands out to receive.

The sultry river wind drowned out my voice as my parents and Linnea rambled by. *Hey*, I shouted. Linnea stopped first, then my white-haired father turned. My little frowning mom, who can't hear too well, especially outside, ears stoppered by the bluster of port breeze and the tourist hubbub and the whap of paddleboat wheels, didn't slow her gym-teacher trot until she noticed she'd walked a good block ahead on her own.

Drago and Klara Cvitanovich, names inscribed into the front of the statue, were what stopped me. We'd met that actual guy, Drago, a grumpy octogenarian in a tropical-print shirt, just the night before, at his oyster joint in a disheveled suburb on high ground at the other end of the city. *Look* at *that*, my father said. Once my mother trotted back she said it too. *Look.* They bent over the name. Drago. We all stared, as if the statue were speaking Drago's name out loud.

Linnea walked around the back of the statue, her polo shirt rippling in the river wind as she bent over to read. Her hair was still long enough to be curly then, rumbling up over her forehead, making her appear a couple inches taller than her actual measure.

I moved in behind her to see where the sculptor had inscribed his name, Franco Allessandrini. One of your people, I said to Linnea. The family laugh breaks across Dad's craggy face. It's an old joke in our family, the Croats versus the Italians. Whatever we might have thought of each other back in the old country, here we were all the children and grandchildren of those long dead Mediterraneans who'd been born with just a sliver of Adriatic between them. My Italian American spouse and I are the last generation likely to keep the joke going.

When I asked Linnea if she'd noticed all the Italian names engraved on the base of the sculpture, she said, You gotta be kidding. There's nobody *but* Italians here. I looked to where she pointed, saw all the names ending in *i*, but also in *ich*. A roster of Croats and Italians ran around the circumference of the monument's base. Except for all those Croats, I said.

The stone roll call left out most of the New Orleans immigrant polyglot. Typical of European Americans to think they are the only ones with an immigration story worth remembering. But sins of omission aside, this was the first I'd heard of Croats coming in not from the Atlantic or Pacific waterfronts but instead from the bottom up, the first of them, it turns out, making landfall before the American Civil War, entering down here through the basement door when the French were still in charge. Some of the Croats who came here in the nineteenth century—to this waterfront, not so different from Croatia's Dalmatian Coast—were sailors who bailed off boats docked in the Port of New Orleans and became the Delta's oyster harvesters, calling their new waterfront property Dalmatia on the Mississippi.

On the other side of the waterfront monument, at the angel's rear, hovering just above Franco's name, looking back into the city, were statues of the prototype European immigrant figures: the bewildered mother, father, son and infant daughter, the boy just old enough to carry a sling over one shoulder, like the boys in any of hundreds of Lewis Hines's photos. Was this Ellis Island or the Bayou? The stone bodies were the standard bundle-and-babushka types, bearers of old stories that have hardened into myths as unyielding as this statue, unbudged even by Hurricane Katrina. Here was an imprecise portrait of our grandmother Kata, her husband Big Petar, and their little boy Petey, not out East but here, in the Mississippi Delta, just a half day's drive along the Gulf from my parents' retirement home.

Allesandrini's stone immigrants, their backs to the water, look bewildered, as if New Orleans were a blinding light. The too easily floodable southern city stretches out before them, the curlicue French balconies and trees dripping magnolia blossoms below sea level, not any home these newcomers recognize. It's too late to choose another route. They've already crossed over.

Overlook: Anniversary View

I wasn't sure I wanted to make this trip to New Orleans. It was my parents' fiftieth wedding anniversary, and for months the family had been arguing. Should we all travel back to Chicago? Book rooms in a resort town, or try for discount cruise ship tickets? Gather at Mom and Dad's golf course? No one could agree. Who would have to travel farther, and which sibling owed which other sibling a visit, and who had more kids to cart around or dogs to board, and which one of us would get stuck with the work if the party happened on our part of the map? If we'd turned out to be one of these families who'd stayed put we could have rented a Chicago South Side Knights of Columbus hall, or we would have set up tables in someone's south suburban garage and rented a keg. Now, instead, everyone was scattered to the four points, and everyone was mad. If you want to find me on my anniversary, my mother said to me when the fighting was at its worst, look in the Biloxi casinos.

Then Katrina hit. The last I heard of my mom's favorite casino it was sitting in the center of Highway 90.

Point of Departure: Anatomical Geography

My friend El and I are sitting in the front seat of her red, step-up-to-ride truck, on the way to a lesbian wedding, when I tell her about Drago. This was before I'd met the guy. My dad had just emailed me to tell me he'd read about Drago's oysters on the Internet.

El and I are both dolled up for the festivities, although *dolled up* is not the right way to describe El. She's in one of her fancy-man suits, looking a bit like Humphrey Bogart. I'm wearing a leopard-print dress and fat-heeled pumps, my ankle and shoulder tattoos showing. El is filling in, at Linnea's request, as my wedding date because Linnea's working the party, best man for her old college buddy Peg, one of the brides. Of the two women getting hitched, Peg seems, to her friends, notably unbride-like, thus her need for not a matron of honor but a best man. Linnea is in charge of event logistics, in-law schmoozing, and stocking the bar. I won't be seeing much of my husband at this shindig.

So I ride to the wedding with El, a transplant from Macon, Georgia, my stand-in date. On the way we chat about Linnea's and my upcoming trip and my family's plans to eat at a Louisiana Croatian oyster house. El doesn't get what I'm saying. What kind of oyster? I'm wondering if El thinks that a lifelong midwestern girl like me doesn't know how to pronounce Creole.

Croatian, I tell her. My father is Croatian American. I know this doesn't mean much to her. It used to be—before the messy Balkan wars and the crackup of former Yugoslavia—people outside our family asked us, Is Croatia some part of Germany? Is it Poland? One of those little provinces obscured by the USSR? Once even I had to work at knowing where Croatia was located on the map, hours spent, when I was in my twenties, staring at atlases, tracing my fingers up around the outline of the blue Adriatic from southern Italy, through Venice and around the bend into the rocky Dalmatian mountains.

Chicago's East Side and Slag Valley are strange even to lifer Chicagoans, unless they're Croatian or Serbian or Polish or Mexican and their people are from there. Unless they know those wooden houses swaying in the wind of Lake Michigan, those steel bridges rising into the mill fog, that rotten-egg stink from the mills. Unless they remember those Croatian taverns like the Golden Shell, with its cevapici, breaded shrimp, and beer, the velvet wallpaper, smoke-smudged mirrors, and big-haired waitresses, the cluttered stage where the tamburitza bands played their skinny-neck Yugoslavian guitars and button box accordions, and where their dads, smiling after a few beers, sing along to some embarrassing polka.

When I say to El, *Croatian oyster*, I mean to convey both memory and dissonance. Like steel city people and Mississippi Delta seafood. Like Lesbian Best Man. Like Peg and Bride. El tries, but she doesn't get it.

TripTik New Orleans: Here's the thing about fiftieth wedding anniversaries. Everyone I talk to from my generation tells me their family turned it into some kind of fracas, an old tradition that used to be fun but somewhere along the way cracked up on a New World shore. The New Orleans trip came about after Linnea and I opted out of the big anniversary argument. No more fighting for us. Instead we offered to meet my parents anywhere, whenever they wanted, as long as we didn't have to get anyone else in the family to agree.

My folks chose New Orleans because it was where they went every May, just six hours' drive west along the broken Gulf Coast. At first

I balked. According to the news, nine months after the post-Katrina floods the French Quarter was open for business. Still, I wasn't sure about taking my parents out to dinner in a ruined city where none of us lived. Would we gawk at all that waterfront property that had been so recently under water? Would we bother those people down there?

When we got to this city where most of the famous restaurants were open and most of the not-so-famous homes were uninhabitable, the locals said, Thank you, thank you for coming, and it seemed like they meant it.

Point of Departure: Matrimonial Crossings

The theme of the lesbian wedding is Etta James's version of the song "At Last." At long last home for two women in their forties. During the testimonials one of Peg's brothers shouts, *It's about time*, and everyone laughs.

It's hot, unseasonably so for May in Minneapolis. My dress is sleeveless, so I'm coping. El is handsome in her neat crew cut and mystery date wedding clothes, but her face is a little too red. I ask, Are you hot?

I'm dying, she admits, which makes me laugh, only because El, wearing Georgia on her sleeve, usually complains she can never get warm enough in cold Minneapolis. So I poke her and ask, Have you finally assimilated?

No, she says, and I flinch at her edge. I ought to know better than to badger people about their geography. Now El will never take off her hot jacket and get comfortable in this airless church basement where both brides are sweating in white satin and hose.

A lesbian wedding is a vortex of both geographical and anatomical crossings. Families cross state lines, cross gender lines. The wedding guests dress every which way. Peg is Linnea and El's butch/Bubba/football buddy, the type who joins them on motorcycle trips, the sort they'd always assumed would be a groom before she'd be a bride. A week before the wedding the Bubbas held a bachelor party. The wives, such as myself, were not invited. There was a cake, I heard later, decorated with a naked Barbie doll, and screenings of 1950s-era burlesque films, from the days, as Linnea described the show, when women weren't afraid to have hips.

When is a bachelor party not really a bachelor party? When the bachelors are neither bachelors nor bachelorettes? When the rituals are pantomimes of the actual rituals of actual bachelors, gestures toward a realm these technical females can't enter, and what's more have no wish to enter? At this bachelor party the plasticized image of the American girlfriend emerged from waves of chocolate frosting, Columbia of the nippleless breasts and crotch as smooth as the bridge of a nose while a stripper—who was young when she made this movie but must be, by now, old enough to be any of these Bubbas' grandmother—bumps and grinds on the home DVD screen, her moves chaste compared to what runs on network TV these days. All this and good steaks and martinis and the endless toasts ribbing Peg about her agreement to do as her bride has asked. She would wear what? A dress?

Every kindergartner knows brides wear dresses. Two brides equal two dresses. But Bubbas like Linnea, a woman who owns more cufflinks than most people's grandfathers, are women to whom clothing is a transcontinental map. I have a picture of Linnea as a baby wearing a lace-hemmed dress, and even then, age two, with her boyish smile and wide-legged gait, she looked like a tourist in the country of girls. Peg, a short wide woman, normally wears jeans and motorcycle boots. The Bubbas feared Peg would end up a stranger at her own wedding.

Yet on her steamy wedding day Peg seems nearly at home in her dress, floor-length, white, a satin sheath billowing from her shoulders to the tips of her shoes, a more tailored version of Columbia's white angel sheath, and what's more, her face flush with a sappy grin, she looks happier than I'd ever seen her. I don't understand the dress, El says to me. You would never ask Linnea to wear a dress, she says. You take pride in Linnea's dress jacket and cuff links and wingtip shoes, she says. I agree. I love Linnea's Italian gangster dress-up clothes.

No one I know would dare ask Linnea or El to wear a dress, but El tells me stories about her family, who love her but refuse to understand why she won't grow out her hair. They once even barred her from a family funeral because she wouldn't put on a skirt. I cringe at the thought of Linnea in a skirt. Early in the planning Peg told Linnea that everyone in the wedding party, according to the wishes of Peg's bride, would wear some kind of skirt. Linnea laughed and said, So you think so?

But citizenship can be a funny proposition. Should traditions cross over to meet the irregular body, or should the irregular body cross over to meet the tradition? Peg's bride sees it one way. Peg's friends see it another. Peg is at home in the middle. The thing about the unconventional woman is even her unconventionality may vary. Sometimes she faces out toward the water, a few shreds of a dress clinging to her breasts. Sometimes she is the one wearing the pants, looking hard into the land.

Overlook: Water View

The thing about waterfront property is, in the real estate ads, the city port view is what makes a property pricey. It used to be the urban waterfront was the back door where the ships came in and the sewage flowed out, but now, instead, it's where to find the condos, lofts, and houses with wraparound decks facing out toward some shore. In Chicago the riverfront, once a graveyard of abandoned warehouses, is now the location of upscale apartments with iron balconies overlooking the river, the same river where nineteenth-century engineers reversed the current to keep the raw sewage from emptying out onto the shores of Lake Michigan.

The thing about cleaned up views of the water is the way water pulls like longing, like craving, like sex. There must be some who stand before the glass, look out at the shore, toward the frothy surf or the clip of the current, shuddering before they turn away. People, for instance, who come from the wars in Croatia or Rwanda, or the floods in New Orleans, where floating bodies lead them to believe the water takes more than it gives. But for the rest of us the shore can be the picture of crossing over, where it all, at last, begins to get better.

The thing about New Orleans is that TV news can't begin to show what happened there. When Linnea and I asked people working in the French Quarter how they were holding on, since the storm, they told us—barely. Their houses were gone. Some got FEMA to give them a trailer, but then they had to wait a month before anyone remembered to hand over a key. The landlords of what was left of livable shelter were kicking people out.

TripTik New Orleans: It's all demolished now, Mom said, practically the first thing out of her mouth when my parents picked up Linnea and me at the airport. All gone. A big flat nothing. Both Mom and Dad shook their heads as they spoke. They couldn't stop talking about the devastation all along the Gulf Coast. My dad's white hair tufted up a bit in the hot wind of the airport parking lot. I noticed my mother was wearing shorts. How hard must it be to try to fix a moldy mess of a house in this climate, where it was already in the nineties in May.

Dad drove us around the city to look. We were no longer worried about gawking because no one was home to see us stare. What we saw caused me to hold my hand over my heart. The French Quarter, the Garden District, all the guidebook locations were on high ground, relatively unscathed, but the neighborhoods on all sides looked like what's left after a war. If the houses were upright they were knocked off their foundations, missing window glass, holes in the roof where rescue workers cut their way in or people trapped in the attic punched their way out. Frayed patches of curtains trembled in the muggy breeze. Dead gray magnolia trees lined the center of boulevards. Cars killed by the water sat in shattered driveways as if the people were still at home, making dinner for the kids, petting the dogs. The people who used to live here had shipped out to Texas, Florida, Minnesota. Some left messages spray-painted on the outside of their house. TONY + MARIA R SAFE—GONE 2 FLA. Nobody was home there, not for miles.

In that old song from *West Side Story*, when Tony and Maria dream of a place, they are longing for not just a room for the night but also landfall, a shoreline. Can you imagine, my mother kept repeating, losing a home like that? Home for my mother is what she's spent her whole life making in order to leave her uneasy sense of homelessness behind.

Overlook: Population View

All those names engraved into the base of Drago's statue, all those Croats, all those Italians—they seem to turn their backs on too many others who make up the city. The African slaves, bought and sold, free or not. The waitresses and cooks in the French Quarter restaurants. The Creoles who used to own the famous brothels. The girls, some of them who used to be boys, circling the late-night streets, smiling slyly at the passing cars. The French military personnel who came to town and never left. The aging gay men with one pierced ear and short shorts who walk the same route every morning for their coffee and news, who'd hunkered down in some pre-Stonewall bar to wait out the storm. The lawyers and the realtors, the city workers and the cops. The carriage drivers and the bartenders. The ones who stayed. The ones who fled. The ones descended from those taken from some other place before they ended up here. The ones who'd never felt at home anywhere else.

A Meandering toward Another Far Better Place

Kata and Petar arrived at some new port, not this one. Their ride was shorter and more direct than the voyages of the Croats who came here one hundred years before, those Dalmatian sailors who traveled around the tip of Africa on their way to New Orleans or Louisiana, island people, seeking cities that shone as well and as bluely as the sea.

When my brother and uncle traveled to old Yugoslavia in the 1980s they found a whole island of people who bore our family name. But my great-grandfather was born in a mountain shack, up a scrubby hillside too rocky to farm. Big Petar was just fifteen, and those were the years young men like him, born to the provinces, were doomed to end up ammunition in the Austro-Hungarian Empire's army. The army may be why Petar and his seventeen-year-old bride hopped the boat. Or maybe he heard the stories, a neighbor or cousin just back from the New World with postcards in his pocket. They wouldn't have known what was in store, blast furnaces spitting out enough soot to blot out the sun, mineshafts like gullets.

When Big Petar, Kata, and little Petey made landfall in the harbor of Baltimore, Petar's grimy hat in his hands, his dirty blond hair lifting and falling in the harbor wind, Kata's hands, already rough from field work, squeezing the hand of her second-born and only living son, they must have thought, Where is it? Squinting and leaning. Tasting the salt air as the squat houses of Baltimore slid into view. Kata may have spotted no more than a smoky tendril rising from a box of red brick. At last.

TripTik New Orleans: At first Linnea and I didn't notice the bathtub ring around New Orleans, or rather we noticed it, but it didn't occur to us what it could be, that sludge-colored line that in some spots was knee-high off the ground, in other spots just below the cracked eave of the roof. The line was the color of rust, the color of slag, what I think of as an old Chicago color because so much of the waterfront property of my childhood bordered the detritus of the steel mills, rusted, abandoned, boarded up. The broken parts of one city look a lot like the broken parts of any other: piles of bent things, wrecked warehouses, shattered glass, splintered wood, waterlogged cars, a junked-up harbor, unmeltable, unburnable debris. The result of human, natural, and industrial disasters looks spookily the same, no matter how it got that way. Except in New Orleans there was more of it than I'd ever seen in one place before.

The New Orleans bathtub line wasn't exactly a line, not a sharp edge so much as a wide, rusty smear, an impression stained into the body of the house, as indelible as a tattoo.

The thing about the people of New Orleans, the lucky ones who were back, is it wasn't hard to get them to tell us their story. This became what Linnea and I did on our vacation: we talked to anyone who met our eyes, asked how they'd weathered the storm.

The woman in the praline shop said she was fine, but business was bad and the woman who worked for her hadn't been right since her home came apart in the flood. The hotel bartender was okay for the moment, but customers were few, her landlord was tripling the rent, and no place cheaper wanted to deal with her dogs. The hotel desk clerk wouldn't be able to fix his house until the electricity in his neighborhood finally came back on, but even now, nine months after the floods, no one from the city could tell him when that would happen. The guy who sold me the used book, Italo Calvino's diary of American cities, said his French Quarter store and apartment were fine, but his friends' houses were wrecked, and the clean-up work, tearing out the mold-infested walls and floors, was no good for anyone's health. The waitress at the restaurant near the courthouse lived on high ground, but the others cleaning up the lunch shift with her—and here she stopped, pointing them out one by one. She lost her house. He lost his. That one's on high ground so she's okay, but this one here lost hers, and she did also, and her—how about you, Honey, are you okay? But him over there, he lost his house too.

Overlook: Flood View

Imagine what it would be like if your city flooded. Imagine it losing hold, this location where you'd found your way. First your carpet is damp, then your shoes. Imagine huddling upstairs with your lover or your kids or your dogs and what little drinkable water you thought to carry up with you. Imagine they tell you the dogs have to stay behind once the rescue workers pull you through the hole in your roof. Imagine spray-painting these words on your siding: MARIA + TONY OK. PLZ SAVE 2 DOGS IN BATHROOM. Imagine later your house is branded with a red X, like the markings of a marauding army, the date search and rescue crews boated by, leaving numbers and code. *1 body. 2 dogs.* DOA. Imagine all your furniture and clothes and family photos vomited out onto the street, your walls furry with mold, and imagine you develop asthma from air turgid with water rot, with garbage no one is paid to pick up, with dead bodies the volunteer workers still haven't found. Imagine your home has such an excellent waterfront view that the water lines stain a rusty measure just below your bedroom windows.

Point of Departure: Geographical Crossings

Minneapolis is a city that's hard to see because it doesn't wear history on its sleeve. All but one of the glass skyscrapers were built in the past two decades. The city's most noticeable waterfront, aside from its cultivated lakes strung together like a blue glass necklace, is the shore of the same Mississippi that runs all the way down to New Orleans, but the river is narrower up here, populated with not riverboats but the shells of flour mills on their way to becoming lofts with waterfront views.

Linnea and I own a house in Minneapolis, as does El. Like us, she bought hers when city real estate was cheap. El rebuilt the inside of her house herself, and the deck too, around which she planted honeysuckle, lilies, strawberries. If I were to describe El as a woman I'd say she's of medium height, medium build—but she's not quite female. As a guy she's on the short side. Her hair, cropped to a curt bristle, is surprisingly soft to the touch, a fact I will discover later on, when Linnea's hair grows back after a head shaving and El lets me run my fingertips over her noggin, to compare.

Although she's not the talkative sort, El's the definitive host. Her perfect portrait would portray her framed in an open doorway. Most lesbian artists I know in Minneapolis have attended parties on El's deck, grabbed a beer out of El's fridge, or, if they're AA members like me, made tea on her kitchen stove. I was among a few dozen women who took off their shirts in El's kitchen the night she turned thirty, accepting a dare to compare brassieres. (We all realized en masse that the early days of lesbian feminism had passed when we saw that most of us were actually wearing brassieres.) It was in El's kitchen, in front of Linnea, during the same session of Truth or Dare, that I kissed a hunky lesbian firefighter on the lips, only to be embarrassed later that summer when that firefighter became one of Linnea's and my neighbors. Since then we've eaten Christmas dinner in El's dining room, told stories in El's living room, shared popsicles on El's deck with a swarm of children and their lesbian moms. When El turned forty we attended a party where El's then-girlfriend performed a 1940s-style pin-up-girl striptease under the backyard honeysuckle. Sometimes I'll be introduced to a woman at another party or art event who seems familiar, and we'll look hard into each other's faces, then laugh and say, Right, I've seen you at El's.

At the time of Peg's wedding El and her lover, the one who'd honored her birthday with such excellent burlesque, had just broken up again. El's on-and-off lover was a traveling theater artist, a woman in love with El but not in love with the way most of us define home. Linnea and I became accustomed to this friend's visits, but no matter how many times you visit a city, visiting is not living. The visiting body grazes, takes off her clothes without ever getting bare. The body who lives here becomes more than naked, opened up and healed over, part of the grit and greenery, whether she comes to love the city or not. That's finally the difference between the tourist and the resident. One might feel the city under her skin; the other is of the city's skin.

At Peg's wedding El tells me her ex-again lover finds home in people, not places. I both understand and don't. Perhaps some of what El fell in love with was her lover's beautiful fleetingness, a body never static, painted toes grazing the water but never falling in.

Who would I be without the skin of a constant city? I have imagined leaving my house with the screened-in porch and brick back patio and my books and collections and two grinning blond dogs and Linnea who still laughs at my wisecracks. I've imagined myself as that girl in a nineteenth-century novel, stepping off a train, a new metropolis inhabiting my hips and thighs like bordello jazz, city lights heaving up around me, the lit-up spires projecting across my chest, like those old films of dancers in jazz clubs, knees and elbows crazy, careening, palms open, faces askew with frenzied smiles.

And then what? A touch? Another marriage? A new home? A glass coffee pot and a checked apron? Sitting alone in a chair, drugged up by a daydream of myself as another body, stepping out of another train, another city, another music inhabiting my hips?

I worry about leaving home. I worry about losing home. El's itinerant lover won't have to worry about her ground washing away. I'm not sure which one of us has it worse, or better.

TripTik New Orleans: New Orleans is not my home, but what I've learned about the city shimmies its hips in me. Both rock-and-roll and jazz is palpable here, and loud, even with so many musicians in exile since Katrina, opposite sounds competing at the cacophonous crossroads of the club district. Palpable on the tongue, in the nostrils, are the smoky gumbos, the blistering jambalayas, Drago's charbroiled oysters. The divides of class and race are palpable, in the ways I remember from my youth in Chicago, particularly on the streets surrounding the French Quarter, tourists circling in air-conditioned cars and service workers hovering in the muggy haze, waiting for broken streetcars that never seem to show up.

The famous voodoo vibe has become, on the surface, a commodified artifact, reformatted to fit the racks of tourist trap storefronts—T-shirt shops, their doors wide open to the street, witchy rock music overwhelming the sidewalks—but the old spells might still reside in the relaxed postures of the locals, black and white and mixed, driving tour buggies or playing horns on street corners for tips, dependent on, oblivious to the gaze of tourists like my family and me.

Beyond the Quarter are neighborhoods that could have been the bombed-out blocks of South Central LA or South Chicago or any disheveled city avenue—these apocalyptic blocks somebody's mortgage, someone's broken box of a life, a street where all these months later no army has arrived to clean up, where stinking post-Katrina refrigerators still sit on the curbs, FREE GUMBO and SMELLS LIKE FEMA spray-painted across the doors.

The absent bodies on these streets are some of the same bodies absent from Drago's waterfront monument, and their absence, in both standing evidence and in the inscriptions of history, is some of what keeps this post-Katrina New Orleans numb. Where is the waterfront statue remembering the sold and liberated slaves? The Creole business owner? The criss-cross Indians who became black and the Africans who became some kind of Indian? The Korean immigrants serving coffee and beignet at Café du Monde? The flood victims? The tranny girl Linnea and I saw from our Dauphine Street balcony, sashaying and swishing until she catches the eye of a man driving a blue pickup and points him to a quiet spot around the corner?

But what keeps this city more awake than most is the way bodies are always palpable, as if the cling of this southern stew collects shadows of all the rendezvous that have transpired here. It was even possible to glide past the Bourbon Street girlie shows in the company of my parents without flinching. My dad was so relaxed in New Orleans he invited Linnea and me out to see the go-go dancers at Harrah's, the emergency police headquarters during the storm now back to its roots as a jittering casino that might be the corporate future of New Orleans.

My dad stood in Harrah's next to his daughter's lesbian spouse, the city humidity crimping Linnea's salt-and-pepper curls, the loose cut of her jeans obscuring, from behind, the technicalities of her gender. My clingy back dress may have been a mistake in all that air-conditioning, the chill a little too palpable across my chest, as I walked past all those slurry-eyed men slumped over their slots. We three didn't so much gawk at the gyrating college girls dancing bare-thighed on the raised pedestals as we noticed they were working hard enough to perspire, burly security guards pacing below, staring down any guy who wandered in too close.

I wondered if Dad had invited us to the casino because in a city like New Orleans he could finally see Linnea as the son-in-law he always imagined for me, a smarty-pants buddy who'd banter about good books, bad Republicans, jazz history, the cultural significance of go-go girls and bars like this one, drink glasses set down in a fog of dry ice, the drinks themselves appearing to be voodoo offerings, while outside, at the waterfront, Miss Columbia stared out over the shore, hair streaming back, breasts welcoming all comers. Her backside sheltered either a promised land or a broken promise. Is this home? At last?

A Meandering toward Another Waterfront Property

When Big Petar and Kata made landfall they stepped right off the boat and onto the train. The B&O Railroad in Baltimore Harbor had special cars for the immigrant workers. Herded in, jerked forward, they headed west.

Once, while traveling for work, I went to the old immigration port of Baltimore to look for the island pier where Kata and Big Petar had landed. I had a few hours' reprieve from a conference. A harried visitors' center clerk pointed across the water. I smiled and said please to the skipper of a water taxi, and he varied his usual slow-season route between the new Marriott and the chain restaurants, all built on landfill that used to be a grimy industrial port remade into visitors-only space, unnatural gatherings delineated by profession—this week creative writing teachers, next week industrial marketers. At the dock of the Locust Point piers I high-stepped over unshoveled snowdrifts, a choreography for which I had not packed adequate shoes. I was looking for my family's backstory. I found a new office park. Train tracks. Old-time taverns. Drago had built no statue here. There wasn't even a plaque.

I walked farther into a neighborhood of brick row houses where no one seemed to be home. A ceramic Madonna shone from one picture window, Our Lady surrounded by plastic roses, evidence of the family life of an old-time company town. But which company? The docks were abandoned. The orange-lit Domino Sugar sign, wide and tall as a semitrailer, shone its blood-orange beacon over the harbor, but the water taxi driver told me that sugar was no longer processed there.

A massive grain elevator shadowed the tight blocks where I walked, in the middle of the street to avoid the snow. I kept walking until the mill was at my back, and only then did I begin to understand why the streets of this neighborhood were so deserted. Parked along the curbs were shiny late-model SUVs, Volvos, and a Lexus or two, in between first one building site then another with billboards that read NEW MULTI-USE PROPERTIES—UNITS START AT $300,000.

Still, a bit of a leftover world was visible here and there. An old white woman with high hair and a yellow babushka slipped down her front steps and stepped into a twenty-year-old white sedan. And some of the taverns had their original signs. Down the Hatch. Bloomers. At Fran and Bill's the sign taped to the window demanded NO LOITERING. Who was around to loiter?

I noticed the ad for a historical calendar published by the local Chamber of Commerce. BUY IT HERE. I walked into Fran and Bill's, a narrow neighborhood joint. The beefy guy behind the clean bar was settled into his seat and looked half asleep. He reminded me of my Polish uncles from my mother's side. Another guy who could be my uncle slouched at the end of the bar in the comfortable pose of a regular. An older dame with ratted hair and wearing a blue windbreaker was working the pinball machine. The bartender was startled when I asked to buy a calendar. Well sure, he said, you can buy them all. It was late February. He had a few left over.

The bartender told me the looming grain mill had closed just that past January. No one knew what would happen to the site. Getting so fancy I can't afford to live around here anymore, the bartender said, which caused him to chortle, along with the regular. Even the broad who pumped quarters into the pinball machine let out a few snorts. Probably make it into waterfront property, the regular at the end of the bar slurred, and they all cracked up.

Before leaving Baltimore I bought a ticket to the Top of the World observation deck of the Baltimore World Trade Center, which the sign in the elevator told me was the tallest five-sided building in the world. *Five-sided* was the key phrase here, because as far as buildings go it was not so tall, just the tallest thing in sight, aside from the Domino Sugar sign.

The music piped in through the speakers was an endless loop of Karen Carpenter singing "Top of the World." From the observation windows looking out over Baltimore Harbor, I could imagine the German steamer carrying Big Petar and Kata and Petey riding in toward the docks. There would have been no beacon advertising Domino Sugar in 1908. No twenty-story hotels or fenced-off patches of gravel marked on the map as sites of future development.

The printed guide said that this waterfront was a no-man's land before the developers saved it, to which, I thought, it must have been *some* man's land. I could make out the finger of ground reaching into the harbor—Locust Point—and the pier pilings where my relations would have stepped off the boat, dizzy, hungry, elated after the nauseating voyage. Most of the immigrants, I'd read, who disembarked here had contracts with the midwestern mills and mines, and so stepped right off the boat and onto those trains, ushered by anxious mine agents, counting heads. From the Top of the World I could see the train tracks I'd walked across the day before, and from that vantage point I walked along the hexagon of windows, tracking the route the train would have taken, away from that waterfront property, deep, deep into the land.

Overlook: Memorial View

Looking at New Orleans after the floods it's not hard to remember that all the glorious old cities in history did eventually die. Ur, Eridu, Babylon, all once the site of functioning governments and religions, once places people lived, are now just archaeology sites, as well as the locations of endless war. Post-Katrina New Orleans might be the start of such crumbling, although, granted, the dissolve might take centuries.

I find I expect the cities to dissolve. Most of the apartments I've lived in since moving to Minneapolis have been torn down. Most of the cars I've driven on the streets of my little city were junked after the last time I drove them. Half of the industrial suburb where I lived during grade school, once a booming company town, is boarded up, abandoned, unsaved. I perpetually expect to turn around and see the geography of my past crumbling like what's left of a tissue paper city after it catches fire.

But in calmer moments I don't expect the cities to burn or drown, and I long to live on high ground, in a loft with big windows, one of the new ones overlooking the old flour mill ruins in downtown Minneapolis with views of the Mississippi curving through the university, then disappearing south toward New Orleans.

But what if all the levees break and the rivers overflow? What if the cities of America are replaced by conference cities, museum cities, Waterfront Property Inc., precious replicas under glass?

TripTik New Orleans: After dinner at Drago's Oyster Bar my dad asked a stranger to take our picture with old Drago himself. Drago nodded without cracking a smile, his bald head bobbing lazily, his bushy eyebrows reminding me of Croat uncles on my father's side. Sure, sure, glad you're here, Drago's posture told us, but if you weren't then some other customer would be sucking up the same air, so please don't take up too much of my time. I stand next to Drago in the snapshot, his arm on my shoulder, my arm on Linnea's shoulder, my dad and mom completing the chain, Dad and Linnea echoing each other's open stance, Dad and Drago wearing similar summer Hawaiian-print shirts, our bodies together a statue of several crossings.

When I tried to talk to Drago he wasn't too interested in my questions. Your oysters, I asked, is this the way they're prepared back on the Dalmatian islands? Sure, sure, he said, but what did he care about what they did over there? Drago was part of New Orleans now, and had been for something like fifty years. Any wars he'd lived through were here. But his restaurant, safe on suburban high ground, didn't flood too bad this time, and business was good.

Point of Destination: High Ground

The unbride-like bride flushes red, happy all the way through her wedding, even as her panty hose shreds from her thighs to her ankles, some crossings only temporary. When I look up from my reception table huddle Linnea is standing behind me with a box of water bottles, her face ruddy with the heat, her short hair curling tighter in this muggy underground. She kisses me on the neck and I lean back into her belt.

When Linnea moves on to deliver more water to the masses I notice, across the table, a woman with a puff of gray-blond hair—she'd come with one of Linnea's motorcycle buddies—watching me. In her silver-blue blouse she looks cooler, and less at home, than the rest of us.

She used to know Linnea, the woman volunteers. They'd worked together once. Some committee at the university. Turns out she'd been listening to my conversation with El, about whether open marriage ever works, about losing love, about what it might take to start over, to date again. The woman must have heard something in my voice, the restless part of me, twenty years married, musing, not as seriously as I must have sounded, but perhaps too loudly. Maybe she thinks I'm flirting with El. Maybe she doesn't get that I'd no more flirt with any of the butch and Bubba relatives than with Nea's Harley-guy brother. Maybe she finds it indefensible that I can't seem to love my home without imagining it gone.

I see now that this woman, despite her ice-blue aura, has anxious eyes, the ungrounded look of someone recently flooded out. By her hard squint I see that she doesn't think much of me. When she said *I know Linnea*, did she mean she thinks she's caught me doing something I shouldn't? And had she? Now she asks, but it's not a question: Why do you wonder about the problems of dating? You're the one who won the lottery.

She's sure I don't deserve my prize. And maybe I don't, but still, I bristle. Yet all I can do is gaze back through her bright blue ice. Say Yes, I know, I'd been lucky so far, all these years on love's high ground.

Overlook: Common Ground

The truth of anyone's marriage is we live our lives more complexly than maps can convey. Let's say we want safety. Or let's say we don't want to get bored. Let's say we don't want to lose it all, but neither do we wish to molder in all that we refuse to lose. People who say we shouldn't rebuild New Orleans, or should rebuild only as a clean theme park, because the place is not safe the way it was, these people are missing the grace of a city made out of all the greed and graft of any city, like Baltimore, like Chicago, yes, but also the city of possibility's dream of itself, the kind of city, like all the best cities, that has to live on the precipice of its own downfall. There will always be some who need to live with, or at least visit, such common and historic cacophony.

When Linnea and I are in New Orleans we steal away from my parents long enough to play. When we move into our own hotel room, built above an old Storyville brothel, we unpack the new toy we brought along, a toy we'll start using here, so much so we'll come to name it the Big Beignet. Love's high ground. Love's low ground. Love's big ground. Love's gritty round. My husband handles what comes inside and I'm louder here than I've ever been before, but this is New Orleans, where nobody cares. The Big Beignet may hurt at first, or startle, but soon I accept, fully, and this mixed and unflinching mapping is what the motion of love's high ground needs to be.

TripTik New Orleans: In New Orleans the difference between high and low ground was palpable. As Dad drove us past the shells of smallish houses I noticed how similar they were to the brown brick bungalow we lived in when I was in grade school, the first home my parents owned. You work your whole life for a home, Mom said, and then what do you do when it's all of a sudden ruined?

I sidled up to Linnea, pressed my arm into hers. We didn't come here to celebrate fifty years of family squabbles. My parents' marriage was their business, but home was another thing.

As Dad drove us into the city, down Canal Street and through the sodden and demolished neighborhoods, I kept one hand on my heart, as if I meant to keep it from spilling out. We are safe among the survivors, celebrating fifty years of some kind of high ground. We are driving by the museum of the end of the world, wondering how to celebrate the longevity of refuge in a place where nobody's left at home.

FIG. 17. *A time table indicating the difference in time between the principal cities of the World and also showing their air-line distance from Washington* by Samuel Augustus Mitchell, 1890.

A map of the city is really a map of time.

City in the Middle

Everyone gets headaches, and some people get worse headaches than these. Linnea's headaches were more than a tension throb, not as bad as a migraine.

Still, we worried the headaches were caused by something growing or pressing or about to burst. This was before we imagined the gray smudge on the MRI, a small gray *thingy* our family doctor told us, with a diameter halfway between that of a nickel and a quarter, maybe growing, maybe not; it would take an expert to know for sure, the kind of doc who knows the brain the way a cartographer knows the route between one city and another.

The MRI of Linnea's brain looked like a map, a flat scan of what's really a globular mass. Impressions that look like roadways or the tributaries of rivers, marking the folds in the tissue, the tumor a round section where the color changed, from smoky white to gray. If her brain scan were a highway map her tumor would appear to be a city, a dead metropolis, soon to be detonated, remade into open space, ready for either regret or development.

We had once been the ones dirty dancing, close to the band, her leather pants, my tight leather mini, the guitar player trying to catch my eye

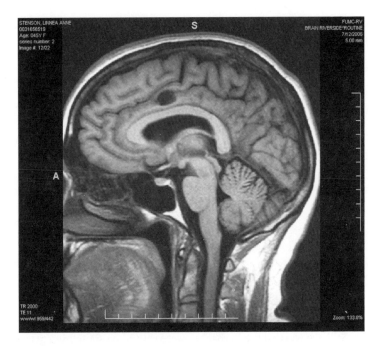

Fɪɢ. 18. The city in the middle of Linnea's brain.

even after I laughed and sidled closer to Linnea. We used to be the ones who'd pulled over to the side of the interstate between Minneapolis and Chicago to make quick love between the shiver of passing semis. Now we were middle-aged, halfway from, halfway there, and a mass growing on the inside of Linnea's skull made her leg twitch and caused headaches so sharp and sudden and sickening she could only lie back and hold her hand over her eyes.

The surgeon told us Linnea's tumor was located in what head experts call *the silent part of the brain*, because it was in the frontal lobe, away from motor and memory. What is the silent part of the brain? Is it a region that can't speak, refuses to speak, or is simply shy, the province of wallflowers and agoraphobics? Or in Linnea's case, her legacy, part

Swedish and part Italian, is the silent region simply her internal Scandinavia, fair-haired and stalwart, able to bear pain, unable to speak up against the wails of all those Italians on her mother's side?

It happened first with no warning, just after we made love, her face fallen into a grimace, her eyes closed. In another era I might have reached for the phone, or called out for help. In another era our lovemaking would have been a secret, so perhaps I would have just gathered her head into my lap and pressed my fingers into the open space of her hairline. In this era I leapt from my bed to get my laptop, typed words into the open entry space of a search engine: severe + headache + after + sex.

Linnea lay back against the pillow. I'm all right, she kept repeating, but she didn't open her eyes as I tapped the keyboard, read lists of worst-case scenarios—aneurysms, blood clots, tumors—making her promise to call the doctor. She nodded but did not get up. It's an impulse of the body, when split apart by pain, to fall back, shield the eyes from light, brace the shoulders, and bite the tongue.

The Linnea I found when the nurses finally let me into her room after the brain surgery wore a patch of white bandage on her head, her bald scalp washed in yellow pigment, yellow like danger, yellow like the sky just before a tornado. But that was just the surface. Inside her head the tumor was gone, scooped out like dollop of ice cream, a watery and distinct mass the diameter of a nickel. Not malignant. The room was pale and dark, the day rainy, the window by her bed looking out over a gravel rooftop. The pewter light discolored everything, the hospital sheets, my right hand on Linnea's chest. She squeezed my left hand. Not hard.

Not that night but the next, I found Linnea's letter. No one needs to explain that reading a good-bye letter from a lover who survived is not the same as reading words left behind by a lover who died. But the letter itself is the same letter it would have been had the unthinkable happened, a hieroglyphics of symbols and ink scratches. The material map is static, but what did and did not happen creates the possibility of two completely different cartographies. A map is accurate only in conjunction with the land it means to represent; if the land changes, so must the map.

I think about grief on late autumn nights, driving west on I-94 after teaching an evening class in Saint Paul. I drive toward the Minneapolis cityscape, and at a certain point the highway seems to turn upward and hover for a moment, as if aiming for the middle of the skyline. The lit-up center of the city is so much wider than it was when I first moved here. Where once I imagined I could hold this skyline in my palm, now I would need at least both hands. If I weren't clutching the steering wheel that's what I would do, grab this skyline with my palms, shake it like a snow globe. It's true the light of the city, freckling the midwestern night with constellations of light, seems to make promises. Come here and your body will be so speckled and bright.

But this light, though actual, is not the truth. Sometimes at night I still drive up close to the skyscrapers downtown, no more than ten minutes' drive from Linnea's and my home, and I look up into the windows. All I ever see is the opposite of what I want. Not a light that engulfs me, immerses me. Not climax. What I see are empty offices. Desks wiped clear for the evening. Dry space, bristling with static. The space of work without the breath of humans working. Not heaven.

Truer is the bump of the pavement under the wheels of my car or the blare of the speakers in the sedan that pulls up beside me, kids with cigarettes, wide-open laughter, the music turned up too loud. I can feel the thump of their bass line in the frame of my own car, in my chest. This is not music I would choose to listen to, yet I turn off the jazz on my own radio because the cacophony is more than I want. I notice here—in the middle of the city, in the middle of the country—the girl in the passenger seat of the other car feeling the flood of smoke in her lungs as she inhales her cigarette. I remember the last time I smoked a cigarette, on a summer evening seventeen years ago, and I remember why I smoked it. I wanted to feel the city under my skin, but which city?

A few weeks before the surgery we asked our friends to help us shave Linnea's head. Our people gathered in the yard. These were twenty years of Minneapolis friends, people who'd come to our wedding, people who'd spent their holidays with us after we stopped driving back to Chicago every Christmas. Some were native Minnesotans, but most were transplants, emigrated to the top of the map for the usual reasons Americans move: for school, for work, for love.

On this sunny October afternoon we gathered, some of us dressed as sexy nurses to make Linnea laugh, the rest simply present, simply attentive. The light of many eyes focused on my hands as I leaned Linnea's head against the faux medical décolletage—a minidress no real nurse would wear, that I wore to accentuate this moment of our bodies surrounded by the gaze of the place we'd lived our lives together, because I could feel my breasts and hips in this dress. I ran my fingers through the dense growth of Linnea's gray curls. Our people watched as I pulled the electric razor through the gray brush, exposing the map of her bare noggin to the sky.

The surgeon and his nurse had told me Linnea might be sitting up in the hours right after the surgery. They said she might even be talking. They didn't tell me to expect her seemingly lifeless body, never described how she would look laid out on a hospital bed, her eyes not opening, her head yellow, like the aura around the middle light of a stoplight.

I was, of course, upbeat when I talked to people before the surgery. We are expecting the best, I said. We are expecting the most positive of outcomes. I was acting as if I were a naturally hopeful person, a person more like Linnea.

The first words Linnea muttered, her eyes closed, her hospital robe falling off her chest, her Mercurochromed head as still as cement: Was it a DNET?

A DNET is the kind of tumor we hoped she had, because it was not cancer, no tails or tentacles left behind that would cause the bugger to grow back, no radiation or chemo needed. We were praying for a DNET, that unassuming collection of sounds and letters that sounded nothing like the name of a brain tumor to me. Most of the tumors had long unpronounceable names. Like *ganglioglioma*. Like *oligodendroglioma*. We were pushing for the one with the shorter, easier-to-navigate label.

I didn't know how to get at the meaning of this DNET we hoped to find nestled in Linnea's head. *Hope* is a funny word to use here, but accurate, because if you are going to have a brain tumor this is the one to have. DNET is actually short for *dysembryoplastic neuroepithelial*, is more common in kids than adults, is slow growing, is the cause of seizures and headaches, is removable by surgery, is not cancer.

Once, as an adult, returning to Chicago, I drove by a famous alderman's house on the East Side, my Gram Rose's old neighborhood. The alderman lived on a block of clapboard houses, but his home was a pumped-up, brick split-level with tennis courts in the back, in a neighborhood where the only other tennis courts were in the city parks, ratty squares of blacktop surrounded by chain link. *De-net* is a sound I imagine coming out of the alderman's mouth as he's running around on that out-of-place tennis court with his grandkids, everything he says pronounced in that old South Chicago accent of my youth. Hit de ball. Over de net.

As the idea of the DNET took shape in my own brain I didn't even bother to memorize the pronunciation of the other tumors. I figured I'd think about the others if it came to that. I'd try to understand Linnea's tumor as this wished-for DNET, a benign, round mass in her head, much smaller than a tennis ball but the same shape, played over an actual and figurative net, this brain surgery a complicated game with equipment and rules and traditions recognizable and yet unfamiliar to us.

Was it a DNET? Linnea asked me, when she felt me sitting beside her. We don't know yet, I whispered back. We have to wait until it comes back from pathology. But it's probably benign. The doctor said. Linnea nodded but did not open her eyes.

It's not so surprising that I thought Linnea might die. I've always worried about her dying. Every time she takes off on her motorcycle.

Every time she goes out with her friends and gets home later than she promised. Every time I ring her phone and no one answers, I think, Oh, maybe she's dead.

When we first got together I'd bypass that *maybe*: She is dead. And my chest would tighten. I wouldn't know what to do with my hands. She's dead and I should call someone, but whom? Linnea's the one I usually call. If my car dies, if I miss the bus, if I'm teaching a night class and have left something important on my desk and need someone to jump in the car to get it to me. How many times has she come out to the shopping center parking lot with her mechanic friend because my crappy old car won't start? How many times has she come home from work in the middle of the day because I'm too sick to drive myself to the doctor?

In the middle of her brain surgery, sitting in the university waiting room, surrounded by something like fifteen lesbians and a few blood family members, Linnea's mom looked over at me and said, *I just had to stop myself from asking Linnea how she thinks things are going. I forgot that Linnea wasn't here.* I was thinking the same. How weird it was to be waiting for Linnea without Linnea here to wait with us, helping us all stay calm.

We did what families always do while the doctors open our lovers' hearts or stomachs or brains. We sat still in the waiting room. My sister-in-law read a novel. My niece did her homework. My friends debated which Catholic saint was the patron of the brain while I used the hospital WiFi to look up hagiographies. We were a jittery and static spiral at the center of a city that didn't stop churning just because our little village was sitting stock-still.

The first time I took Linnea back to Chicago with me to meet my family we had dinner in a restaurant in Greektown. Outside the restaurant windows the city skyline leapt straight up out of the flat black top of Greektown valet parking. Downtown Chicago from the west is the backdrop of the first portrait of my family that includes Linnea. The Pegasus valet must have taken it. Little Grandma, my parents, and one of my brothers, Benny, who still lived with Mom and Dad then, while he was in law school, are all present in the shot. Linnea wears her black leather jacket. I'm in skinny jeans and a red knit pullover sweater vest that I'm surprised I wore because it had been a gift from a previous lover.

Linnea didn't mind me wearing clothes some other lover had given me, even after I made her stop wearing the diamond earring stud left over from her former lover. She didn't mind that the motorcycle she owned then used to belong to my former lover too, nor did she mind that I'd ridden on the back, behind a woman I'd kissed, long before Linnea had owned the bike or kissed me. And she didn't mind when Little Grandma told her, when we mentioned that Linnea had a motorcycle, about the neighbor boy who'd crashed his motorbike right into the wall of the hospital. Of all places. This might be where I got it, from my mom's side of the family, the expectation of disaster, this constant film loop of motorcycles plowing into hospital walls, of lovers vanishing. Even Little Grandma expected Linnea to die on me.

We asked, but they didn't know where brain tumors came from. Not from power lines. Not from the city water supply. Not from cell phones or microwaves or UFO abductions. The same percentage get brain tumors today, in 2006, the doctors told us, as had them in 1964. Our friends say, No, no. It has to be the cell phones. It must be that garbage burner nobody wanted. It's the toxic dumps that used to rim the South Side of Chicago. It must be some city's fault. Others, the ones who've lost someone, shrug, speak of our time of life, remember when none of us thought we'd live even this long. This then is the obstructed view from the middle, at the intersection of ambition and the body. What if we cross into no city at all?

Before Linnea's brain surgery, and during, and after, when she might have died, or if not died then never reentered behind her eyes, or once reentered still never able to speak more than those first dead-end turns—*It's good, Okay, Love you*—my comfort was to picture who

I might become in some alternate city. I'm not talking noble widow here. I painted myself happy in other homes, not our wooden house and mottle of rosebush but a smooth loft hovering over the Mississippi, Lake Michigan, the Pacific. Dragging up narrow steps to a slight room in Manhattan. Closing the blinds of a Chi-town brownstone. Watering potted plants on a terrace in San Francisco within view of a blood-orange bridge.

In the letter Linnea left she'd written me free. *Love well*, she wrote. *Love widely*. Did she know what I'd already conjured? The new lover and I on a stone bridge of some downtown, the city rising behind us like a pearl curtain, gaunt thighs and hard arms holding me from behind, woman or man or some body in between. I don't know what kind I would love or even fuck after twenty years faithful to Linnea, so I pictured all kinds, full-breasted and flat, maybe fingers, maybe phallus, likely silicone, possibly flesh. The betrayal is not that I thought of other bodies but that some moments, tired of waiting, I even hoped for them, not parked loss but the open map, another beginning, unmediated blue.

Then again I didn't know I would love cupping Linnea's bare head in my palm, feeling the sharp shadow of new hair against my skin, that I would love running my thumb against the creases and indentations that I never knew were there. I have, more than once, held the bare head of a baby in my hand, but never before the bare head of an adult. It's an unusual intimacy, tender but also electric. I could feel both her distress and her light scratching the lines of my palm, her head an illumined globe. I recognized Linnea, the same person she had been in the twenty years we'd loved each other, but also, unveiled to me this way, she felt new.

Great-Grandma Kata may have felt she was headed to no place, on a train trundling from the edge to the middle, the child who would be my grandfather Petey snoring in her lap. I hope Kata at age seventeen felt as hopeful as I did at her age, the tug of a train pulling her forward, her body crisp, bent toward the future. On their long train ride from Baltimore to the Michigan copper mines, they would have had to change trains in Chicago. The city may have been the biggest she'd seen. I imagine Kata taut at the sight of the limestone peaks and spires, the silhouette of the gray city causing her to catch her breath, one hand pressed against the base of her throat, one squeezing her son's shoulder until he squirmed free.

Seventy-five years later Gram Rose, the one who would marry that little boy in Kata's lap, drove her blue Chrysler away from Chicago, eighteen hours south to a plot alongside a snaky green corridor littered with golf balls. For twenty-five years Rose walked her new world every day she was able, white hair puffing and fluttering in a muggy southern breeze, her feet in neatly laced sneakers. In her last months she talked of those shimmering numbers above a door on Michigan Avenue. One of the last times I walked the golf course with her she described those downtown doors to me as if they were the entryways of both her youth and her final passing, as if she hoped to walk through them again soon.

Middle City Interlude: The commonness of mortality may be its most excruciating beauty. I stretch out on our living-room couch, my thighs swung open, my hair loose, my blouse partly undone. When Linnea looks my way I run my finger over the hollow where my breasts begin. She finds my eyes and smiles. As usual, our oldest dog, Dusty, notices when Linnea and I start to get going. She tries to insert herself in between, sixty-five pounds of blond fur in my lap, trying to stop what she knows is coming next, the guttural sounds of Linnea and my shared geography. As usual, I coax Dusty to the cushions behind my head and then Linnea is the one between my knees, one hand unsnapping my bra, one hand unzipping my jeans, my fingers stroking the scar just under her hair, but lightly, because I don't want her to flinch. The approach is always the same, always brand new. We scale the hill. We see the city in its entirety and the light contains us. I peak and then extinguish into her hands. Again. Again. This is the life I migrated toward, the city where I have chosen to live—*this* is what it means to live in the fully conscious city.

By the time we enter the city in the middle, the intersection of the dream city and the real, we see the place we end up might be no place. Driving back west into Minneapolis at night, Linnea's reckoning one year past, I notice the blue speckle of downtown. I stared at that skyline each morning I drove between home and the hospital to see Linnea. Now I think, This is the city where Linnea had a brain tumor. The city where my love wrote me a good-bye letter and then didn't leave, where I lost not marriage, but a familiar way to fold our old highway map, a still legible geography that won't ever fold flat again. Our bodies are maps of a city where twice, at least, we've started again, no longer young, still bent toward some kind of arrival.

FIG. 19. *Chicago of To-day. The Metropolis of the West. The Nation's Choice for the World's Columbian Exposition*, Acme Publishing and Engraving Co., 1891.

A bird's-eye view of a possible city.

The Middle West as My Body

She trudges westward, across the prairie, Our Alternative Lady of Midwestern Midlife, one of America's bodies. She is walking the old glacier trail. She is bent forward into the wind. Her hair is cut in a 1920s bob, the hair of a woman who wants to be free of the past. Her eyes are ringed with slag-colored kohl, and the toenails of her bare feet are painted an industrial shade of purple. Her thighs are wide and bare, and her arms and shoulders too, except for the tattoos, an amber rose, the head of a leopard, a luminous skyline merging cities, one old and one new.

She wears red urban cowboy boots from the 1970s, a leather mini-skirt from the 1980s, a leopard-print push-up bra from the 1990s. She wears the fingerprints of both men and women. She wears an estrogen patch just above her left hipbone. Separating her breasts is the strap of a leather bookbag, in which she carries the names of all her former lovers and all the body insults—like *cunt*, like *drunk bitch*, like *unnatural woman*—ever aimed at her eyes or her breasts or her belly, and postcards of all the cities she has visited but never lived, such as Rome, Reykjavik, Venice, Tokyo, and a thermos of strong coffee and a wrapper of dark chocolate, and memory fragments scribbled on the backs of bar napkins.

Where old Columbia threaded the West with power lines this girl leaves a trail of silken flower syllables denoting the body—bristle of bald scalp and spongy tissue of brain and bird of tattooed breast and pink rope of belly scar and cradle of inner thigh. Around her the country is in its usual uproar. The *Empire Builder* has finally fallen off its tracks. The freeways are jammed, bumper to bumper, and airplanes circle her head like gnats. The bombs of unceasing wars keep blasting, but we can't hear them from here. It's unclear if our lady is an invader, an immigrant or a citizen, a conqueror or a returnee, a good witch or a bad. Ahead, just past the poppy farm, the blue city is her beacon. She is leaning forward, pushing west, all the way feeling she is entering the outskirts, beyond which she'll find something big, something shimmering, the American dream, or some believable facsimile. Her body is the map of the voyage from there to here, the record of her travel. She is headed for the city where, since cities began, women have journeyed in order to transform themselves from good girls to bad, from fallen woman to the woman next door. When she gets there, the new country, her life will be common, but all the way there she feels mythic.

FIG. 20. Aerial view of Sears Roebuck, Lake Street, and Elliott Avenue, Minneapolis, 1928.

My bird's-eye view of the city that remains.

Body Geographic

Linnea is getting a new tattoo. What had been our uncut bodies are scarred now. The hysterectomy left a cross-city highway across my middle, and Linnea's marking traverses the top, under a bristle of gray, what had been a tumor now a prairie lot in her brain. Linnea is adding a full back piece this time, to commemorate living. Something blue.

What had been a stretch of used car lots and pawnshops is changed now too, not just the part of town where the aging hippies and midlife lesbians live, but also the Spanish- and Somali-speaking city, a locus of twenty-first-century Middle American immigration. Lake Street today is a long run of taquerías and supermercados, Mexican bakeries and shops selling hijab of many colors, along with the indie coffee shops and renovated bowling alley bars where lesbians and computer geeks and postpunk off-the-gridsters mingle.

And Lake Street has tattoo parlors, the younger generation shops with clean picture windows and koi ponds and the tattoo artists' oil paintings crowding the walls.

Both Linnea's and my first tats, dating back now almost twenty years—my right-shoulder leopard head, the hummingbird over her heart—are the work of an old-timer named Spider, a wiry biker dude who was always talking, always smoking. We had to drive forty-five minutes out of the city to see Spider, back in the days when the only tattoo parlor within city limits was run by that other guy, the one known to stare at women's breasts too long.

Spider's dead now. A hard-party guy, he'd had a heart transplant back in the 1980s but kept on living so close to the edge he wore out the second heart too. Since then tattoos have become the uniform of urban youth, queers and bohemians of all generations, a way for us to claim our bodies as self-ruled territory.

Linnea's new domain is a blue geography. A Japanese waterfall with a rocky backdrop and leaping koi. Japan is not our territory, just the first overseas country Linnea and I traveled to together, the year Adria was born, in Tokyo, and the first country Linnea ever wanted to visit when as a child she imagined the places she might go. Water, Linnea tells me, because change is inevitable and we can't step into the same river twice. Koi because the word is a homonym for love and because the blood-orange koi is a fish said to accept the adversity of the knife without a quiver. And cherry blossoms because they are a flower of transience evoking the fragility of life.

Linnea's current tattoo artist is Kurt, a skinny guy wearing loose jeans and a faded T-shirt, the same dude who will later tattoo Chicago and Minneapolis over my tailbone. We didn't have to leave the city to find him. He hand-sketched the landscape onto Linnea's back, with marker. I held Linnea's hand as Kurt leaned over her shoulders, the tattoo gun buzzing, her flesh flooding with rapids of blue ink. When he finished Linnea was a map, but not of where we've been nor where we're going, but rather where we choose to locate, between the thighs and the shoulder blades, on the rocks, within the water, in the holy, damaged corners of our brains and always blue under my hands.

Above the buzz of Kurt's ink gun, through the picture window, westward, is a gray tower, the old Sears building, the main floor an international market, the top floors new loft condominiums called, as if after my heart, the Chicago. Atop the tower are green lit-up letters that read, simply, MIDTOWN. Our Lady of Lake Street flashes green back over where we started and westward toward wherever any of us might end up.

I frequent a gay-run coffee shop just off Lake Street where recently I sat next to two lissome men no older than twenty, touching each other across the table, leaning close for kisses, their conversation sliding between accented English and Somali, so engrossed in one another they didn't notice me eavesdropping. One wore baggy black drawstring pants, a black buttoned shirt with a turned-up collar, and huge white Jackie O sunglasses, even though it was night. The other was dressed gay urban casual, shin-length jeans, brown slide-on mules, a striped T-shirt. They mentioned one of the state colleges about thirty minutes outside of the city. They must be, I thought, some of the first from among the East Africans newly arrived in Minneapolis to attend an American university, not to mention the first young men in their immigrant families to kiss other young men in American city coffee shops.

One of the young beauties was quizzing the other for a geography exam. *Plate tectonic*, Jackie O offered, and his rounder, more serious-looking lover recited back: *Oceanic and continental crusts colliding*. To which Jackie O began to sing: *Oceanic, oceanic, oceanic*, then *Continental, continental, continental*, loving the sounds of words as well as worlds. Come on, his lover said, I have to do this, and Jackie O read the next term from a spiral-bound notebook. *Symbiosis*. His lover replied, *One cannot exist without the other*, then added, Like you and me. If I died you would drive into walls. No, no, said Jackie O. I would drink the poison. He made a drinking motion with his hand, and they both laughed. What a world, what a world, Jackie O sang, and I thought, Yes, what a world, plates of rock and bodies floating, colliding, geographies killing and surviving, blue cities singing, all our maps continually making and remaking.

Outside was a blustery May evening, and when I walked the block south, back to Lake Street, I saw, eastward this time, the green-lit Midtown sign. From the Midtown tower the view of downtown's glass and light mountain range is said to be spectacular, but I do not see the overview from Lake Street. From ground level all I can do is ride in a car, bike, or city bus or walk. Forward. After the ones who came before, leading the ones who will come after. Midtown is an accurate geographical coordinate, the intersection of Chicago Avenue and Lake Street, close enough to the perfect middle of Minneapolis—but that any life has a natural midpoint is a myth. If Linnea had died at forty-five she would have passed through her Midtown before we'd even met. If I live as long as my ninety-six-year-old grandmother my Midtown marker is now. Still, our ideas of midlife are a useful delusion, a faulty yet practical coordinate that might help keep any of us on our feet.

Every night, at the midpoint of Lake Street, the Midtown tower flickers green, and every day under Linnea's suit coat a waterfall tumbles, and always under our feet the earth inches around a constant axis, oceanic and continental crusts colliding, the tower at the center peering down on our place. The middle.

FIGS. 21A AND 21B. *Rand McNally & Co.'s Minnesota (with) Minneapolis, St. Paul and Vicinity,* 1903.

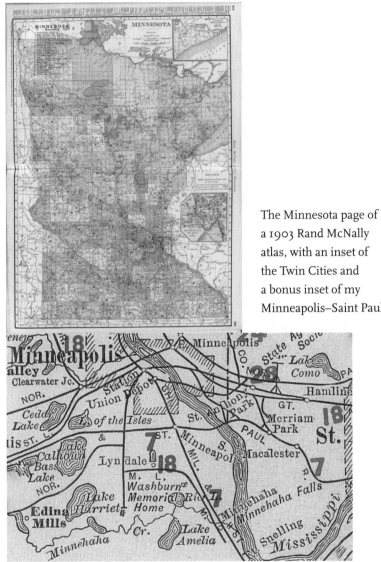

The Minnesota page of a 1903 Rand McNally atlas, with an inset of the Twin Cities and a bonus inset of my Minneapolis–Saint Paul.

About the Maps

Maps embody time as surely as—in fact because—they embody space. DENIS WOOD, *Rethinking the Power of Maps*

Anyone who opens an atlas wants everything at once, without limits—the whole world. This longing will always be great, far greater than any satisfaction to be had by attaining what is desired. JUDITH SCHALANSKY, *Atlas of Remote Islands*

I have come to consider this book a variety of map art—my own quirky attempt at countermapping my American body against the "true and accurate atlas" any woman of my place and generation was supposed to follow. Yet this project did not begin in the literal form of an atlas. Rather my first drafts were fragments about the intersections of place and the body, most particularly the juncture of my body and the far South Side Calumet region of Chicago inhabited by both sides of my family for as long as they have been Americans. My generation, as some of the first in my family to leave Chicago and the last to remember family members born in Europe, are naturally too the first to have reason to consider how the industrial Midwest made us who we came to be. This mix of memory and curiosity carried me well past genealogy into immigration history, world's fair chronicles, and urban studies, which then led me into the ephemera and images of history archives, and then finally, viscerally, to maps, where I could not help but notice all of the above coming together in visually arresting ways.

How many times have I stared into a map of Croatia, in search of some ineffable origin, hoping to pinpoint the tiny village where my grandfather was born, the homeland his family later fled? How many times have I run my finger along the map lines of Chicago, the homeland I fled, in an attempt to comprehend the relationship of the neighborhoods where I grew up to my parents' and grandparents' neighborhoods, to the long drive through Wisconsin postprairieland, to the Minnesota city where I have for three decades made my New World home? I came to the map as narrative form midway through this writing, but maps themselves have been my talismans since long before I began this particular book.

Maps don't solve the mystery of why environment and human longing are so intricately intertwined, but something of the way maps bring together embodied landscape, documentary inquiry, and artistic subjectivity has worked to enhance, and make corporeal, my understanding of all my places. Similarly the act of lyric and narrative mapping brings me closer to an understanding familiar to any personal essayist or memoirist, which is that renderings of the self are no more than attempts or—as the critical cartographer and map artist Denis Wood describes maps—propositions. The best we can do is map in a manner that embodies the invisible beauty of spatial comprehension, which is what the maps I include in this book, my own and those of others, each in their fashion, strive to achieve.

List of Illustrations

Fig. 1. *Americam utramque: aliis correctiorem* by G. van Keulen, 1700s. Note in this map of the Americas that the female body—Miss Columbia, I presume—stands on the top of a world balanced on the shoulders of Atlas. Courtesy of the Library of Congress, Geography and Map Division.

Fig. 2. *Map of Europe as Queen* by Sebastian Munster, 1570. Note on this map that the Slavic lands of my family make up the lady's belly. Courtesy of Barry Lawrence Ruderman Antique Maps, www.RareMaps.com.

Fig. 3. *American Progress* by John Gast, 1872. This painting is also known as *Manifest Destiny*, *Spirit of the Frontier*, and (irony unintended) *Westward Ho*. This is the first image that comes up when Googling the term *Manifest Destiny* and certainly, as viewed today, illustrates the concept in terms compatible with contemporary progressive understandings of colonialism and empire. Courtesy of the Library of Congress, Prints and Photographs Division.

Fig. 4. *The Man of Commerce: a chart showing the resemblance between the arteries of commerce, as represented by railroads, and the arterial system of man; also, the resemblance between the great vital organs of man and the commercial system of the Great Lakes*, designed and copyrighted by A. F. McKay, 1889; Land & River Improvement Co.; Rand McNally & Co., Engravers. This map makes clear the similarities between cartographic and anatomical art. From the American Geographical Society Library, University of Wisconsin–Milwaukee Libraries.

Fig. 5. *Thornton Quarry, Thornton, Cook County, September 17, 2003*, from *Revealing Chicago: An Aerial Portrait* by Terry Evans (Abrams, 2005). As the history of mapping is bound to the history of aerial photography—bird's-eye-view maps predating aerial technology for centuries, but perfected once human air travel was possible—it's easy to view Evans's photographs as a kind of map. For more of these images, go to www.edelmangallery.com/evans.htm. Courtesy of Terry Evans.

Fig. 6. *Souvenir Map of the World's Columbian Exposition at Jackson Park and Midway Plaisance, Chicago, Ill, U.S.A.*, 1893, compiled and drawn from actual official data by Hermann Heinze, chief draughtsman, Surveys and Grades Department, World's Columbian Exposition. The Museum of Science and Industry in Chicago's Hyde Park neighborhood is all that remains of the Columbian Exposition. Courtesy of the Library of Congress, Geography and Map Division.

Fig. 7. *Chicago in Silhouette* by Howard Lyons, first published in the *Chicago Sun-Times* on April 26, 1959 (the precise date of my birth), and republished, with the rest of the photographs in this series, in *Real Chicago: Photographs from the Files of the Chicago Sun-Times* (Chicago Sun-Times, Inc., 2001). Courtesy of the *Chicago Sun-Times*.

Fig. 8. *Bohemiae Rosa* by Christoph Vetter. A map of Bohemia in the shape of a rose, from Bohuslav Balbín's work of national history and geography *Epitome historica Rerum Bohemicarum* (1668). The rose was the emblem of two powerful families in southern Bohemia. The mixed grace of this image fits my grandmother well, as does its story about power. Note, though, that the rose has Prague at its center and the blossom is rooted in Vienna, the capital of Imperial Austria— an allegorical façade masking a more vulnerable and colonized truth. I believe Gram (who passed away in 2007) would have liked to have seen herself named in association with such rare and unusual cartographic beauty. I came across this image first on Frank Jacob's *Strange Maps*, bigthink. com/blogs/strange-maps. I located an original version in Minneapolis, within the James Ford Bell Library's rare books, maps, and manuscripts collection. Courtesy of the University of Minnesota Libraries.

Fig. 9. *Nineteenth Precinct, First Ward Chicago* by William Stead, from *If Christ Came to Chicago: A Plea for the Union of All Who Love in the Service of All Who Suffer* (1894). Stead was a fervent social activist and sensationalist journalist whose work often focused on prostitution and other forms of late nineteenth-century urban vice. This map may have been the precursor to Jane Addams's sociological maps of ethnicity in the late nineteenth-century West Side immigrant neighborhoods of Chicago. An interesting side note: Stead died on the *Titanic* in 1912. Photo courtesy of the Newberry Library, Chicago. Call# Case F548.5 s8 1894.

Fig. 10. *Map of California Shown as an Island* by the Dutch cartographer Johannes Vinckeboons, 1639. One of many maps created by Europeans between the seventeenth and eighteenth centuries mistaking the west coast of North America for an island. Courtesy of the Library of Congress, Geography and Map Division.

Fig. 11. Ebenezer Howard's *Group of Slumless, Smokeless Cities* is from the classic urban planning text originally published as *To-Morrow: A Peaceful Path to Real Reform* (1898), later republished as *Garden City of To-Morrow*. The original edition was republished in 2010 by Cambridge University Press. Two garden cities were built in England using Howard's plans, and many other developments worldwide were influenced by this work, though critics dismissed his ideas as unrealistic fantasies. I find his city diagrams charming but too controlling, more like a resort than the mess of a real city. © British Library Board. Reprinted with the permission of Cambridge University Press.

Fig. 12. Sanborn fire insurance map of the Trumbull Park Homes, 1947. Sanborn mapped over 12,000 American cities and towns, and their archives contain over 1.2 million maps dating back 130 years. Chicago—1905–1951, vol. 48, 1947–Apr. 1950, sheet 29 (1 page). Reprinted and used with permission from the Sanborn Library, LLC.

Fig. 13. Hales & Hunter Feed Mill, Riverdale, Illinois. The abandoned grain mill we called the Rat Factory is, as of this writing, still standing in the industrial prairie west of 140th and Stewart, diagonally across from my family's former home in Riverdale, just south of the Chicago city line. A 2010 city planning document from the current mayor of Riverdale refers to this structure as "an unresolved eyesore and monstrosity for the community of Riverdale for decades and decades" and requests funds to demolish the building (www.villageofriverdale.org/vrpepo.pdf). But unrealized plans to raze the Rat Factory have been on the neighborhood agenda for decades. I visited the site myself in 2003 and again in 2012; both times I was astonished to find these ruins still in place. Photo by Christopher Allen. Used with the permission of the photographer.

Fig. 14. *My Father Wanders*, 1969. This photograph was taken by my father, Robert A. Borich, during one of the family's many summer road trips, first with a tent trailer, then in a truck camper, and finally in one of those combination truck-trailers called a MiniHome that my younger brother later drove when he worked as a wedding DJ. The map charts one summer's TripTik. Courtesy of the author.

Fig. 15. *Islandia* by Abraham Ortelius, 1587, from *Theatrum Orbis Terrarum* (Theater of the world), the world's first bound atlas of uniform map sheets. © British Library Board.

Fig. 16. *Mississippi River Meander Belt* by Harold Fisk, 1944, from the series of fifteen maps titled *The Geological Investigation of the Alluvial Valley of the Lower Mississippi River*. These maps are part of a technical report created for the Army Corps of Engineers, a beautiful series that tracks the lower Mississippi, every map in the collection just as gorgeous as this one, all of them online and in the public domain. Courtesy of the Army Corps of Engineers Engineering Geology and Geophysics Branch.

Fig. 17. *A time table indicating the difference in time between the principal cities of the World and also showing their air-line distance from Washington* by Samuel Augustus Mitchell, 1890. This image is part of an astonishing online archive of the map holdings of David Rumsey, who put his vast collection online rather than donating them to a university archive because he wants the maps to be easily accessible and well used. Courtesy of the David Rumsey Map Collection, www.davidrumsey.com.

Fig. 18. This is the actual MRI photograph of my spouse Linnea Stenson's brain, taken in the summer of 2006 at the University of Minnesota. Used with the permission of Linnea Stenson.

Fig. 19. *Chicago of To-day. The Metropolis of the West. The Nation's Choice for the World's Columbian Exposition,* Acme Publishing and Engraving Co., 1891. This is the image that first got me thinking about the figure of Columbia and her relationship to the midwestern American city. Used with permission from the Chicago History Museum/Archive Photos/Getty Images.

Fig. 20. Aerial view of Sears Roebuck, Lake Street, and Elliott Avenue, Minneapolis, 1928. Sears Roebuck built this store in south Minneapolis in 1928, and the site was a retail and catalogue location until Sears vacated the neighborhood in 1994 to focus on its suburban Mall of America location, leaving the building abandoned and boarded up for a decade. Minneapolis artists occasionally used the space during that time. The documentary photographer Wing Young Huie mounted mural prints on the side of the building in 2000 as part of his *Lake Street, USA* public art exhibition, and in 2003 my friend Wendy Knox directed a riveting Frank Theater production of *The Cradle Will Rock* in one of the appropriately gritty empty warehouses. The building reopened in 2006 as the vital Midtown Global Market, a project of a coalition of business, community, government, and nonprofit groups. Courtesy of the Minnesota Historical Society.

Figs. 21a and 21b. *Rand McNally & Co.'s Minnesota (with) Minneapolis, St. Paul and Vicinity,* 1903. The additional inset is my close-up of the same map, focusing on the vicinity of my longtime home and work life. Courtesy of the David Rumsey Map Collection, www.davidrumsey.com.

Figs. 22a and 22b. *County & township map of the state of Illinois (with) Chicago and vicinity* by Wm. M. Bradley & Bro., 1890. The additional inset is my close-up, focusing on the Calumet region, where I grew up. Courtesy of the David Rumsey Map Collection, www.davidrumsey.com.

Fig. 23. *Map of Cook County, Illinois, with inset of map of Chicago* by Walter L. Flower, 1861. This map, with its multiple and various scattered insets detailing both location and history, appears to me as akin to the form of a segmented essay on the subject of place. Image no. ICHi-27578. Used with the permission of the Chicago History Museum.

For a color slide show of all the maps in *Body Geographic*, please visit Barrie Jean Borich's author site at www.barriejeanborich.com.

FIGS. 22A AND 22B. *County & township map of the state of Illinois (with) Chicago and vicinity* by Wm. M. Bradley & Bro., 1890.

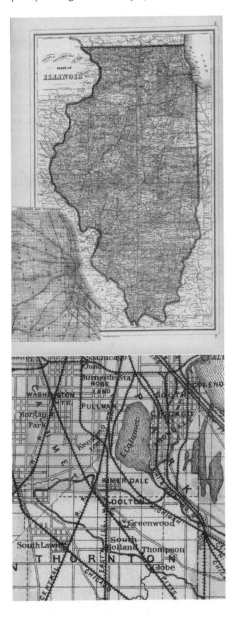

Illinois, from an 1890 Mitchell's atlas, featuring an inset of Chicago reaching into Indiana, with my addition of another area of detail that provides a closer look at the Calumet region, including my family's old neighborhoods of South Chicago, Irondale, Riverdale, and South Holland.

Map of Acknowledgments in which the latitude and longitude of my debt to others is charted.

This book absorbed many years of my writing and thinking life, the territory of my attention including, and reaching far beyond, a great many books, films, archives, websites, museums, classes, critiques, and conversations with friends, students, and family members—most of which I attempt to map here.

Underlays of the Books I read in support of this project, which I did not read as a geographer, nor a literary or cartographic critic, nor a historian. Nor was my research particularly scholarly. Rather, because I am a personal essayist, I researched essayistically, following associations and humoring distractions with glorious inefficiency, usually unsure what I was looking for but most of the time convinced that everything I encountered was related.

I list here selected texts that had the greatest (though usually indirect) impact on the book I finally wrote, rather than the reading that led me toward the many other books I imagined writing along the way. There are countless others, including a few that found no place in this project but that I hope to return to someday, including pattern books for Polish immigrant lacemaking, the letters and memoirs of the Slovenian immigrant writer and radical Louis Adamic, and articles about world's fair fan dancers, to name just a few.

On Chicago

Algren, Nelson. *Chicago, City on the Make.* Chicago: University of Chicago Press, 2001.

Cahan, Richard, Michael Williams, and Neal Samors, eds. *Real Chicago: Photographs from the Files of the Chicago Sun-Times*. Chicago: Chicago Sun-Times, Inc., 2004.

Celander, Charles. *Chicago's South Shore*. Charleston sc: Arcadia, 1999.

Dreiser, Theodore. *Sister Carrie*. Critical ed. New York: Norton, 1991.

Evans, Terry. *Revealing Chicago: An Aerial Portrait*. New York: Abrams, 2005.

Grossman, James R., Ann Durkin Keating, and Janice L. Reiff, eds., with cartographic editor Michael P. Conzen. *Encyclopedia of Chicago*. Developed by the Newberry Library with the cooperation of the Chicago Historical Society. Chicago: University of Chicago Press, 2004.

Miller, Donald L. *City of the Century: The Epic of Chicago and the Making of America*. New York: Touchstone, 1996.

Pacyga, Dominic A., and Ellen Skerrett. *Chicago City of Neighborhoods: Histories and Tours*. Chicago: Loyola University Press, 1986.

Sellers, Rod. *Chicago's Southeast Side Revisited*. Charleston sc: Arcadia, 2001.

Sellers, Rod, and Dominic A. Pacyga. *Chicago's Southeast Side*. Charleston sc: Arcadia, 1998.

Spears, Timothy B. *Chicago Dreaming: Midwesterners and the City, 1871–1919*. Chicago: University of Chicago Press, 2005.

Stead, William T. *If Christ Came to Chicago*. Chicago: Laird & Lee, 1894.

Viskochil, Larry A. *Chicago at the Turn of the Century in Photographs: 122 Historic Views from the Collections of the Chicago Historical Society*. Mineola ny: Dover, 1984.

On Croatia, Yugoslavia, and Immigration History

Erlich, Vera St. *Family in Transition: A Study of 300 Yugoslav Villages*. Princeton nj: Princeton University Press, 1966.

Prpic, George J. *The Croatian Immigrants in America*. New York: New York Philosophical Library, 1971.

Stolarik, M. Mark, ed. *Forgotten Doors: The Other Ports of Entry to the United States*. Philadelphia: Balch Institute Press, 1988.

Violich, Francis. *The Bridge to Dalmatia: A Search for the Meaning of Place*. Baltimore: Johns Hopkins University Press, 1998.

West, Rebecca. *Black Lamb and Grey Falcon: A Journey through Yugoslavia.* New York: Penguin Twentieth Century Classics, 1994.

On Hong Kong, New Orleans, San Pedro,
and Cities in History and Literature

Baum, Frank. *The Annotated Wizard of Oz.* Edited by Michael Patrick Hearn. New York: Norton, 2000.

Hall, Peter. *Cities in Civilization.* New York: Pantheon 1998.

Howard, Ebenezer. *Garden Cities of To-Morrow.* Cambridge MA: MIT Press, 1965.

The Lost Village of Terminal Island. DVD. Directed by David Metzler. Culver City CA: Our Stories, 2006.

Love Is a Many Splendored Thing. DVD. Directed by Henry King. 1955; Century City CA: Fox Video, 2000.

Morris, Jan. *Hong Kong.* New York: Vintage 1997.

The Naked City. VHS. Directed by Jules Dassin. 1948; New York: Kino Video, 2000.

Piazza, Tom. *Why New Orleans Matters.* New York: Harper Perennial, 2005.

Rose, Al. *Storyville, New Orleans, being an authentic, illustrated account of the notorious red-light district.* Tuscaloosa: University of Alabama Press, 1974.

On Maps, Mapping, and Geography

Baynton-Williams, Ashley, and Miles Baynton-Williams. *New Worlds: Maps from the Age of Discovery.* London: Quercus, 2006.

Harmon, Katharine A., and Gayle Clemans. *The Map as Art: Contemporary Cartographers Explore Cartography.* New York: Princeton Architectural Press, 2009.

———. *You Are Here: Personal Geographies and Other Maps of the Imagination.* New York: Princeton Architectural Press.

Holland, Robert A. *Chicago in Maps: 1612 to 2002.* New York: Rizzoli, 2005.

Jacobs, Frank. *Strange Maps: An Atlas of Cartographic Curiosities.* New York: Viking Studio, 2009.

———. *Strange Maps: Cartographic Curiosities* (blog). Big Think. http://bigthink.com/blogs/strange-maps.

Tuan, Yi-Fu. *Space and Place*. Minneapolis: University of Minnesota Press, 1977.

Valentine, Gill. *From Nowhere to Everywhere: Lesbian Geographies*. London: Psychology Press, 2000.

Wood, Denis, with John Fels. *The Power of Maps*. New York: Guilford Press, 1992.

———. *Rethinking the Power of Maps*. New York: Guilford Press, 2010.

On the Tallgrass Prairie Hinterlands

Cronon, William. *Nature's Metropolis*. New York: Norton, 1992.

Evans, Terry. *The Inhabited Prairie*. Lawrence: University Press of Kansas, 1998.

Madson, John. *Where the Sky Began: Land of the Tallgrass Prairie*. Ames: Iowa State University Press, 1995.

On World's Fairs and Images of Columbia

Appelbaum, Stanley. *The Chicago World's Fair of 1893: A Photographic Record*. Mineola NY: Dover, 1980.

Bolotin, Norman, and Christine Laing. *The World's Columbian Exposition: The Chicago World's Fair of 1893*. Champaign: University of Illinois Press, 2001.

Rydell, Robert. *All The World's a Fair: Visions of Empire at American International Expositions, 1876–1916*. Chicago: University of Chicago Press, 1984.

Shaw, Marian. *World's Fair Notes: A Woman Journalist Views Chicago's 1893 Columbian Exposition*. Lakeville MN: Pogo Press, 1992.

Warner, Marina. *Monuments and Maidens: The Allegory of the Female Form*. New York: Atheneum, 1985.

Inset in Which I Acknowledge the Necessity of My Students, especially all those who participated in the many iterations of my Geography of

Memory course, as well as my Reading and Writing the City course (both at Hamline University), and especially all my *Water~Stone Review* assistant editors who repeatedly fished me out of my oceans of papers and files—Michelle Janssens Keller, Beth Duncan Windler, Ahyico-dae, Sarah Turner, Stephanie Olson, and Katie Muggli. Thanks also to Nuria Sheehan and Vanessa Ramos, the MFA students who helped me plan and carry out the public interviews about writing from place with the visiting authors Terry Tempest Williams and Suzanne Antonetta.

Inset in Which I Also Acknowledge My Minneapolis–Saint Paul Colleagues, most notably everyone teaching in The Creative Writing Programs at Hamline University, led by director Mary Rockcastle, with particular thanks to my collaborator and confidante Sheila O'Connor, as well as, for bringing some of this work into her undergraduate creative writing classroom, my colleague and friend Katrina Vandenberg. Thanks to fellow far South Side Chicagoan photographer Laura Migliorino for her help prepping the *Bohemiae Rosa* map, as well as for my author photo. Thanks also to Kate Kysar for asking me to write about my mother for her anthology *Riding Shotgun* and for all she does for the Twin Cities Literary Community, and of course to our good old girl BERTHA, my longtime writing group, which in her most recent iteration includes Judith Katz, Morgan Grayce Willow, and Ellen Lansky.

Inset of the Equally Essential Far-Flung Literary Friends, Colleagues, and Networks who in one way or another helped this book happen (more important, helped me happen), including, most personally, Mary Cappello, Cheryl Strayed, Brian Teare, Suzanne Antonetta, Lynette D'Amico, and Polly Carl.

I'm grateful to everyone at the Rainier Writing Workshop, especially Judith Kitchen and Sherry Simpson, who both read more drafts than any writer deserves; Peggy Shumaker, who introduced me to the University of Nebraska Press; Kevin Clark, whose "dangerous" prompt led me to my turning point paragraph; Stan Rubin just for being himself; fellow travelers Kate Carroll De Gutes and Katrina Hays; my little work group of creative nonfictioneers, made up of Bill Capossere, Jaimie Hays Hartter, Julie Riddle, and Eric Gnezda; and too many other talented, beautiful people to list here. Special love to Theresa Bakker and Andrea Henchey for our geographically unlikely cross-decade alliance that could have occurred in no other space and time.

In the literary world at large I thank Dinty Moore and Judith Barrington, all the organizers of NonfictionNow, all the writers I have not already mentioned who helped my thinking through their participation on my NonfictionNow and AWP conference panels about intersections of place and the body, including Achy Abejas, Harrison Candelaria Fletcher, Rigoberto González, Paul Lisicky, Andre Perry, Bao Phi, David Shields, Ira Sukrungruang, Kekla Magoon, Ander Monson, Ann Pancake, and Lydia Yuknavitch, and all the mighty women of VIDA, who remind me daily of the political implications of women's bodies. I am grateful to Ben George at *Ecotone* for editing notes on "Geographical Solutions" that turned out to be key to revisions of the book overall. And I thank my literary agent, Malaga Baldi, for her faith that this odd book would find a home, as well as UNP editor Kristen Elias Rowley and everyone else at the press for their beautiful and attentive work.

Underlay of Cartographers, Geographers, and Urban Historians (both the professionals and those who collect and remember cities as an act of love) whose work gave me a visual and intellectual focus when I was lost in my material. I am deeply grateful to the geographer Roger Miller for allowing me to sit in on his spring 2006 Changing Form of the City course at the University of Minnesota. Sadly Dr. Miller lost his life in a 2010 long-distance motorcycle trip, so I will never have the opportunity to thank him personally for his thrilling lectures, my response to which led me to the phrase "Cities of Possibility." I wish for Professor Miller eternal rest in some Garden City of To-morrow. Thanks also to Carl Durnavich for his independent work preserving the history of

Riverdale, Illinois, and for sending me the short documentary—years before the film showed up (uncredited) on YouTube—created by Peter and Joe Seely in 1992 for the Riverdale Centennial Commission that compiles the history of the Hales & Hunter Grain Elevator (a.k.a. the Rat Factory). Special thanks to Rob Sellers and the Southeast Chicago Historical Museum, whose website, Chicago's Southeast Side, proved invaluable on more than one occasion, and who led me to the Sandborn fire insurance map of my mother's Trumbull Park Homes. And thanks to both Mr. Sellers and the Chicago State University geographer Mark Bouman for offering tours of southeast Chicago's old steel mill terrain. While unexpected events of the body documented in this book forced me to cancel those plans, the questions developed in the planning process were a considerable help, and I hope future projects will allow my return to these landscapes. Special thanks to the citizens of post-Katrina New Orleans who spoke so openly to Linnea and me, making the loss of their city even more palpable than the ruins of the city itself. And thanks to Katharine Harmon's first volume of map art, *You Are Here: Personal Geographies and Other Maps of the Imagination*, for the idea of acknowledgments as another form of map.

Panorama View of the Formal Archives, History Museums, and Historical Societies, as Well as the Websites and Listservs of Independent Historians where I encountered more of the plain literal stuff of creative nonfiction than I will ever find excuse to use. These include the Immigration History Research Center at the University of Minnesota, the Chicago History Museum Research Center, the Chicago Architecture Foundation, St. Nicholas Croatian Catholic Parish in Pittsburgh, the University of Pittsburgh Archives Service Center: Archives of Industrial Society, the Croatian Ethnic Institute in Chicago, the Riverdale Historical Society, and the Riverdale Public Library. Thanks to Timothy Johnson and Margaret Borg at the James Ford Bell Library at the University of Minnesota for locating the *Bohemiae Rosa* map in their rare books, manuscripts, and maps collection.

Inset of Literary Journals whose editors published stand-alone essay versions of the following:

"Geographical Solutions" appeared in *Ecotone* (Fall 2009).

"Alabaster City's Gleam" appeared in *Hotel Amerika* (Spring 2010).

"American Doll" appeared in the *Florida Review* (Winter 2010), where it was awarded the Editor's Prize in the Essay.

"Mapping the Body Back" appeared in the *South Loop Review* (Fall 2010).

"On a Clear Day, Catalina" appeared in *Crab Orchard Review* (Summer 2010), where it was awarded the John Guyon Prize in Literary Nonfiction.

"Cities of Possibility" appeared in *Water~Stone Review* (Fall 2007).

"When We Were in the Projects" appeared in the anthology *Riding Shotgun: Women Write about Their Mothers*, edited by Kathryn Kysar (Saint Paul MN: Borealis Books, 2008).

"Navigating Jazz" appeared in the *Indiana Review* (Fall 2010).

"Waterfront Property" appeared in *New Ohio Review* (Spring 2010) and was reprinted in the anthology *American Tensions: The Literature of Social Justice*, edited by William Reichard (Oakland CA: New Village Press, 2011).

"The City in the Middle" appeared in *Seattle Review* (Winter 2010).

Bird's-Eye View of My Families, who provided me love, attention, permission, and contexts and answers to myriad questions about the past, particularly my parents, siblings, and in-laws, who accepted my constant absorption in work, and in some cases put up with finding themselves in that work. Thanks also to my south Minneapolis chosen family supper club for the sustenance and nourishment, and especially to El Savage for reading the section in which she appears and gently suggesting corrections, and Morgan Thorson, whose choreographic and performance work opens my mind to new considerations of conceptual sources as well as the ways bodies might occupy, manipulate, and reinvent spaces.

Fading memories of the city where I was born
(with insets of history and monuments).

Inset Note on My Use of the Names of Family and Friends, which are in this work sometimes actual, sometimes invented for the sake of either narrative clarity or the comfort of those who have not asked to appear on these pages. The family members I never met, some of whom do not, to my knowledge, even appear in any family photographs, are characters I created from the fragments of family story and my own imagination. All the rest of the people, places, and events are accurate representations, to the best of my memory, except where my speculations are noted.

Compass Rose of Linnea, still my lesbian husband and my most dear immediate family—along with our canine companions, the Blondes, Miss Dusty Springfield and the recently departed Miss Rosemary Clooney (who left us as I was completing the edits on this book). Though my work takes me far afield—at this writing, away from Minneapolis to a new teaching job back in Chicago—you remain my home, my country, my environment, my most reliable and imaginative map. Thank you, Linnea, for this Theater of the World we share.

In the American Lives Series

Such a Life
by Lee Martin

Turning Bones
by Lee Martin

In Rooms of Memory: Essays
by Hilary Masters

Between Panic and Desire
by Dinty W. Moore

Sleep in Me
by Jon Pineda

*Works Cited: An Alphabetical
Odyssey of Misbehavior
and Mayhem*
by Brandon R. Schrand

Thoughts from a Queen-Sized Bed
by Mimi Schwartz

*My Ruby Slippers: Finding Place
on the Road Back to Kansas*
by Tracy Seeley

The Fortune Teller's Kiss
by Brenda Serotte

*Gang of One: Memoirs
of a Red Guard*
by Fan Shen

Just Breathe Normally
by Peggy Shumaker

Scraping By in the Big Eighties
by Natalia Rachel Singer

In the Shadow of Memory
by Floyd Skloot

*Secret Frequencies: A
New York Education*
by John Skoyles

The Days Are Gods
by Liz Stephens

Phantom Limb
by Janet Sternburg

*Yellowstone Autumn: A Season of
Discovery in a Wondrous Land*
by W. D. Wetherell

To order or obtain more information on these or other University
of Nebraska Press titles, visit www.nebraskapress.unl.edu.

OTHER WORKS BY BARRIE JEAN BORICH

My Lesbian Husband

Restoring the Color of Roses